Psychoanalysarium

In this unique volume, four experienced psychoanalysts present in-depth case studies of child psychoanalysis, highlighting the praxis, development and relevance of psychoanalytic work with children.

Psychoanalysarium – a word that encompasses work, space, time, movement, dream, creativity, *rêverie* and fantasy – takes the reader on an intimate journey of psychoanalytic work through the book's four case studies. The vast clinical material delves into themes such as transgenerational trauma, learning difficulties, sibling rivalry and aggressive tendencies, as well as the impact of separation anxiety and depression in childhood. The different analytical tools used with each child – from drawing to elements of play therapy – allow for a better understanding of, and connection with, children's suffering. This book provides the reader with essential perspectives to expand their own clinical work with young people. Highlighting both the importance of the external setting and the analyst's internal setting, the aesthetic dynamism of the analytical process reveals the complex working relationship with children and the benefits of the psychoanalytical approach.

This book is a vital contribution to the theoretical-clinical field of psychoanalysis with children and will be of interest to all psychoanalysts, psychotherapists and psychiatrists who work with the psychological suffering of children and their families.

Ana Belchior Melícias is a psychoanalyst based in Lisbon, Portugal. She is a full member of the Portuguese Psychoanalytical Society (PPS) and of the International Psychoanalytical Association. She is also a child and adolescent psychoanalyst. She is a former vice president of the PPS board and president of the APOBB (Portuguese Association of Bick Infant Observation).

Isabel Quinta da Costa is a psychoanalyst and full member of the Portuguese Psychoanalytical Society and of the International Psychoanalytical Association. She is also a child and adolescent psychoanalyst. She is a full member of the Portuguese Society of Psychoanalytic Group Psychodrama.

Elsa Couchinho is a psychoanalyst and full member of the Portuguese Psychoanalytical Society and of the International Psychoanalytical Association. She is also a child and adolescent psychoanalyst. She is also supervisor of multidisciplinary teams in the context of residential homes for children and youth at risk.

Raquel Quelhas Lima is a psychoanalyst and full member of the Portuguese Psychoanalytical Society and of the International Psychoanalytical Association. She is also a child and adolescent psychoanalyst. She is also a child and adolescent psychiatrist, focused on primary health care and child psychiatry liaison.

The Routledge Child and Adolescent Psychoanalysis Book Series

Editor: Christine Anzieur-Premmereur
Co-Editors: Mary T. Brady, Christine Franckx and Fernando M. Gómez

The Routledge Child and Adolescent Psychoanalysis Book Series is devoted to manuscripts that illuminate the creative and challenging work of child and adolescent psychoanalysis and psychoanalytic psychotherapy. While we believe that the study of child psychoanalysis is relevant to all psychoanalysts – as the study of the unconscious is essential to all psychoanalysts – the particularities of child and adolescent work require that the setting adapt itself to the child and adolescent, not the other way around. We also see children and adolescents as quite sensitive to cultural and societal changes and catastrophes. Children and adolescents are like the canaries in the coal mine – particularly vulnerable to the presence of gases. For that reason, our Book Series is dedicated to excellent and creative clinical technique and theoretical work, writing that is sensitive to the setting, and writing that is perceptive of societal and cultural changes that affect children and adolescents.

The series editors are especially interested in selecting books which enhance the understanding and further expansion of infant, child, and adolescent psychoanalytic thought. Part of the mission of this international series is to nurture communication amongst psychoanalysts working in different models, in different languages, and in different regions of the world.

Series Editor Biographies

Christine Anzieu-Premmereur is a psychiatrist and psychoanalyst in New York City who works in private practice with adults, children, parents and their babies. A member of the Société Psychanalytique de Paris, she is on the faculty of the Columbia Psychoanalytic Center for Training and Research and is Assistant Clinical Professor in Psychiatry at Columbia University. She is the chair of the IPA Committee for Child and Adolescent Psychoanalysis (COCAP). With Vaia Tsolas, she is the co-founder of Pulsion Institute. She recently published *The Process of Representation in Early Childhood* and *Attacks on Linking in Parents of Young Disturbed Children*. She co-edited with Vaia Tsolas *A Psychoanalytic Exploration of the Body in Today's World: On the Body* (2017) and *A Psychoanalytic Exploration of the Contemporary Search for Pleasure: The Turning of the Screw* (2023).

Dr. Mary Brady is an adult and child psychoanalyst in private practice in San Francisco, USA. She is on the Faculties of the San Francisco Center for Psychoanalysis and the Psychoanalytic Institute of Northern California. She is Editor of *Braving the Erotic Field in the Treatment of Children and Adolescents* (2022). Her books, *Analytic Engagements with Adolescents* and *The Body in Adolescence* were published by Routledge in 2018 and 2016 respectively. She is North American Co-Chair for the Committee on Child and Adolescent Psychoanalysis (COCAP) of the IPA. She co-leads a Psychoanalysis and Film group.

Dr. Christine Franckx is an adult and child psychoanalyst and psychiatrist. She works in Antwerp in private practice for adult analysis and she has created an analytic psychotherapeutic center for early development (0–6 years). She is a Training Analyst of the Belgian Psychoanalytic Society, of which she has been the President (2016–2020). She is Editor of two books *Eros op de scene* (2021) and *Het kinderlijk trauma* (2023). She is trainer in Infant observation (Esther Bick). She is European Co-Chair for the IPA Committee on Child and Adolescent Psychoanalysis (COCAP).

Dr. Fernando M. Gómez is a child and adolescent psychoanalyst, psychiatrist and pediatrician. He works in Buenos Aires in private practice for children, adolescents and adults analysis. He was trained at the Asociación Psicoanalítica Argentina (APA), of which he has been Director of the Publications Committee (2016–2020) and of the Department of Children and Adolescents "Arminda Aberastury" (2020–2023). He is Latin American Co-Chair for the IPA Committee for Child and Adolescent Psychoanalysis (COCAP). He is a member of the Advisory Council of the General Directorate of Mental Health of the Government of the City of Buenos Aires. He edited a 4 volumes collection: *Pilares del Psicoanálisis Contemporáneo* (2017, 2018, 2019, 2020), *Psicoanálisis Contemporáneo Latinoamericano* (2017, coedited with FEPAL), and he is currently editing *Clinica e Investigación en el Psicoanalisis de bebés, niños y adolescentes. Nuevos horizontes, nuevos desafíos*.

Titles in the Series

Psychoanalysis with Adolescents and Children
Learning to Surf
Mary T. Brady

Child and Adolescent Psychoanalysis in Times of Crisis
War, Pandemic and Climate Change
Kristin Fiorella

Psychoanalysarium
Four Case Studies of Child Psychoanalysis
Ana Belchior Melícias

For more information about this series, please visit: www.routledge.com/Routledge-Handbooks-in-Religion/book-series

'Creativity (. . . even in the title!), theoretical and clinical competence, depth of thought and openness to the new and to complexity are just some of the characteristics of this fascinating and valuable book, which, through four very lively clinical cases, accompanies the reader into the area of child analysis and then, much further, into the infinitely vast area of the childhood basis of adult life. *Psychoanalysarium* is a very useful tool for all those who work in this field, and confirms how psychoanalytical therapy for childhood psychological distress has made progress that was unthinkable until a few years ago.'

Stefano Bolognini, *Former President of International Psychoanalytical Association*

'This is one of those rare books demonstrating how deep is the psychoanalytic practice.

An homage to child and adolescent psychoanalysis, this is a manual on child analysis, demonstrating how the analyst maintains the analytic process, through 4 detailed analyses of children of different ages. As Virginia Ungar pointed out in her foreword, the child analyst is in touch with the reality of the unconscious fantasy. The complexity of transference and countertransference is explored and gives rise to fascinating elaborations on psychoanalysis with children. This is a brilliant book, exciting and very accessible: a good combination of education and psychoanalytic thinking. This book is an essential theoretical and clinical document for adult and child analysts, and for everyone in analytic training.'

Christine Anzieu-Premmereur, *MD, PhD, Assistant Clinical Professor in Psychiatry at Columbia University. Chair IPA COCAP (Committee for Child and Adolescent Psychoanalysis), Co-Founder New York's Pulsion Psychoanalytic Institute*

'Four children . . . four psychoanalysts and their inspiring trajectory masterfully captures the very essence of contemporary psychoanalysis: diversity, pluralism, and contemporaneity. It is far more than a theoretical exercise; it's a vibrant demonstration of psychoanalytic practice, skillfully weaving together the wisdom of classical psychoanalytic thought with the cutting-edge of contemporary research. What truly sets this book apart is its ability to transcend the specific focus on children. The reader immersed in the intimate and transformative analytical journeys, will gain invaluable insights into the nuances of the therapeutic relationship with patients of any age!

This book is an essential resource for anyone seeking a deeper understanding of psychoanalytic practice. The authors have created a work that is both intellectually stimulating and deeply moving, a testament to the enduring power of psychoanalysis in our ever-evolving world.'

Sergio Nick, *Former Vice-President of International Psychoanalytical Association*

Psychoanalysarium

Four Case Studies of Child Psychoanalysis

Edited by Ana Belchior Melícias

Authors
Isabel Quinta da Costa
Elsa Couchinho
Raquel Quelhas Lima
Ana Belchior Melícias

Routledge
Taylor & Francis Group

LONDON AND NEW YORK

Designed cover image: © imageBROKER/Wolfgang Weinhaeupl

First English edition published 2026
by Routledge
4 Park Square, Milton Park, Abingdon, Oxon, OX14 4RN

and by Routledge
605 Third Avenue, New York, NY 10158

Routledge is an imprint of the Taylor & Francis Group, an informa business

First **Portuguese** edition published by Freud & Companhia, 2017
Second **Portuguese** edition published by Freud & Companhia, 2024
First **English** edition published by Routledge 2026

ISBN: 978-1-032-95261-1 (hbk)
ISBN: 978-1-032-90197-8 (pbk)
ISBN: 978-1-003-58401-8 (ebk)

DOI: 10.4324/9781003584018

Typeset in Times New Roman
by Apex CoVantage, LLC

To children
To parents
To masters and mentors

Epigraph

. . . the Unicorn . . . was going on, when his eye happened to fall upon Alice: he turned round instantly, and stood for some time looking at her with an air of the deepest disgust.

"What – is – this?" he said at last.

"This is a child!" Haiga replied eagerly, coming in front of Alice to introduce her, and spreading out both his hands towards her in an Anglo-Saxon attitude. "We only found it to-day. It's as large as life, and twice as natural!"

"I always thought they were fabulous monsters!" said the Unicorn. "Is it alive?"

"It can talk," said Haiga, solemnly.

The Unicorn looked dreamly at Alice, and said "Talk, child."

Alice could not help her lips curling up into a smile as she began: "Do you know, I always thought Unicorns were fabulous monsters, too? I never saw one alive before!"

"Well, now that we *have* seen each other," said the Unicorn, "if you'll believe in me, I'll believe in you. Is that a bargain?"

"Yes, if you like," said Alice.

Lewis Carroll (1872). Through the Looking-Glass and
What Alice Found There. Illustrations by Sir John Tenniel.
London: Macmillan & Co. 1996. Chapter VII:
The Lion and the Unicorn, pp. 152–153.

Contents

Epigraph   *x*
Foreword   *xii*
VIRGINIA UNGAR

Introduction   1
ANA BELCHIOR MELÍCIAS

1   **The girl from the sea: The transformation of illusion into
    development**   6
    ISABEL QUINTA DA COSTA

2   **Died, slept, dreamed: From immersion in sensoriality to the
    possibility of thinking**   29
    ELSA COUCHINHO

3   **The ghost of a thousand ghosts: From the hunger of a
    thousand babies to the progressive possibility of symbolization**   40
    RAQUEL QUELHAS LIMA

4   **From scribble to sphinx: Originary phantasies as a
    symbolic matrix**   59
    ANA BELCHIOR MELÍCIAS

    About confidentiality   103
    RAQUEL QUELHAS LIMA

Biographical notes   *105*
Index   *108*

Foreword

Virginia Ungar

The publication of this book is to be welcomed. It is a significant contribution to psychoanalytic practice with children. Its authors are four Portuguese psychoanalysts who have come together to share their daily clinical experiences and generously open the door of their offices to let us see how they work with their young patients. They do so in a way that evokes in the reader an interest, fascination, and passion for the practice with children.

Today, we know that the task enriches our knowledge about young patients' development and subjectivization processes and refines our instrument for working with patients of all ages. It provides us access to forms of communication of a very primitive nature and also to what verbal language often fails to convey. In this sense, we professionals open the way to observe and consider what has not been able to be symbolized; we are in the territory of the nonverbal. In the four clinical experiences that the authors share with us, we can witness these experiences.

In the Introduction, Ana Belchior Melícias makes an important clarification when she refers to the fact that although the four authors have a common affiliation from an institutional point of view, they are supported by a working model based on pluralism articulated with the theory of complexity, which invites readers to accompany them on their journeys enriched by differences and contradictions.

It reveals that they have not been guided by any unifying pretensions from a theoretical or technical point of view, but the guiding idea has been to show each analytic couple in their *psychoanalysarium*. The latter term was created by the editor to refer both to the experiences in the analytic room and to the analyst's mental environment, the potential space of each analytic pair, and the aesthetic point of view of each developing analysis.

In this same chapter, Ana traces succinctly and excitingly the history of child psychoanalysis.

She convincingly shows the impact on the psychoanalytic theory of little Hans's famous visit to Freud together with his father, Mr. Graaf, not to mention the first European child analysts and the renowned discussion between Melanie Klein and Anna Freud recorded in the article Symposium on Child Analysis (1927).

From my point of view, we could say that Freud's initial contact with his adult patients suffering from hysteria showed him the way to the idea of transference as resistance and repetitive recollection of the past.

By observing and then treating children, Klein was in touch with the immediacy of psychic reality from the outset. Reading the Kleinian works, which provide clinical examples from the analysis of her young patients in the 1920s, one finds that transference has a strong presence and power.

These patients indeed found a responsive analyst with an exceptional capacity for observation and improvisation. It is possible to follow this in Klein's contact with each patient, which helped her build on and improve her theoretical ideas while throwing up new lines of inquiry. It is exciting to follow her through her reasoning about the technique she had just created, trying to remain faithful to Freudian doctrine and develop new technical devices at every step.

One of Ms. Klein's disciples and the originator of the Psychoanalytic Method of Infant Observation, Esther Bick, made an important contribution in her article on child analysis (1941). In it, she raised the question of the emotional tensions and gratifications (internal and external) that the practice of child analysis implies for an analyst.

She underlined the tensions arising from countertransference phenomena, saying they are more serious for a child analyst than those acting on an adult analyst. She said that two factors are involved in this process: the possible unconscious identifications of the child analyst with the patient's parents and the nature of the child's material and its mode of expression.

In a child's treatment, the analyst must take action and be personally and physically involved. Bick argues that the nature of the child's mind imposes a greater dependence on the child analyst's unconscious to provide clues to the child's play and nonverbal communication.

If we were to single out Bick's most crucial argument for encouraging psychoanalysts to practice child analysis, we would like to recall her claim that child analysis gives the therapist greater conviction about the reality of unconscious fantasy than working with adults.

To conclude the introduction, Ana Belchior Melícias carries out a detailed analysis of the most relevant contributions to child psychoanalysis from various international perspectives. She also expresses her appreciation of contemporary authors whose reflections and innovations enrich scientific research and provide guidance in complex contexts.

In the book's first chapter, we have the opportunity to share detailed clinical material of enormous value to accompany Isabel Quinta da Costa in an analysis of an eight-year-old girl whose motives are conflicts about separation and sleep. This therapy shows us from the outset all the difficulties that a child therapist can face in establishing a working alliance with adults who can guarantee the continuity of a treatment to a certain extent.

The analyst had to organize an appropriate setting in order to carry out the therapy, as the grandmother made the initial consultation without consulting the parents.

With the patience and determination that her position as an analyst gives her, she established this, working beforehand with what we could call different "transferential factors" coming from her parents and grandmother. She was thus able to access a multitraumatic history of mourning. This way, she managed to "clear the field" and make space for the patient.

From her testimony, the readers are able to witness progress in the child's levels of symbolization. Despite the premature interruption of therapy, they ended on good terms, which always leaves the door open for a possible return.

In the second chapter by Elsa Couchinho, the author takes us on a long journey from the patient's three years of age to her eleventh year and highlights the importance for her of the dynamics of her countertransferential reactions in the initial phase of therapy. She tells us that somnolence predominated in her position as the analyst, indicating that the treatment occurred in the sensory domain at that time. This experience, working with the child and with bimonthly meetings with the parents, evolved toward the possibility of symbolizing and finding narratives through play.

The author finds an interesting and creative way to symbolize her experience in this treatment by using the model of Dante's *The Divine Comedy* to explore scenarios and modalities of the circles of Hell and Purgatory. Thus, she names three periods of analysis as dead, sleeping, and dreaming.

The third chapter, presented by Raquel Quelhas Lima, narrates the analysis of a four-year-old boy who fails in the process of symbolization, with the hypothesis that he did not have an adequate continent function due to the severe depression of his mother.

The analyst presents detailed clinical material from the sessions with the child and also narrates periodic meetings with the young patient's parents. This allows us to see the importance of working with the parental couple, especially in situations such as those that accompanied the child's early life, in which the mother went through a severe depression that included suicidal ideation. This period occupied the first two years of the child's life. They also had another daughter who was seven months old at the start of treatment.

The reason for consultation was a great aggressiveness on the part of the child toward his little sister and his parents, in addition to fear of noises, fear of elevators, nightmares, and nocturnal enuresis.

The account of this therapeutic experience abounds with detail and allows us to witness an evolution from the near impossibility of staying in the playroom and playing with the analyst. By sustaining the analytic attitude, the latter offered a space for the transference to unfold.

In reading the chapter, we accompanied the therapist in creating a space for play, drawing, and dialogue that had to be built.

Also, this account shows the importance of monitoring transference-countertransference in order to access everything that the little patient is unable to express through symbolic language.

Another detail that the analyst highlights and that deserves to be mentioned is the importance she attaches to the help she received from her supervision group. This is a privileged space because, beyond any theoretical differences, this is where we all meet in our daily clinical practice.

The fourth chapter, written by Ana Belchior Melícias, presents a history of an analytic process with a six-year-old boy who starts an analysis because he has critical socializing difficulties. Both parents referred to traumatic family life histories as background.

The author offers a very interesting point of view by focusing the clinical exposition on the theme of the original fantasies, which have been present since Freudian work and are continued by several authors, among which Laplanche and Pontalis stand out. Ana presents her hypothesis that the original fantasies can be thought of as a symbolic matrix and thus allow the figurability of emotional experience on three levels: historical, object, and the functioning of the analytic couple in the psychoanalytic process.

This theme coincides with a personal interest of mine since I have considered infantile fantasies as a system of beliefs, which, of course, is changeable and liable to transform as the subject encounters the mystery of the object. In this sense, they have a defensive character; in this case, the defense is against not knowing. When referring to theories or belief systems, I include the infantile sexual theories about the mystery of the anatomical sexual difference (2022), the family novel related to the mystery of the origins, and the primary scene about the oedipal exclusion, all close to our analytical clinic. In these cases, the psyche is concerned with elaborating fantasy beliefs in an attempt to deal with the anguish that emerges in the face of the uncertainty of the subject confronted with the mysteries of their origins.

To return to the clinic in Chapter 4, it is necessary to go through it to see the progression of the analytic process in terms of the abundant sequences of drawings from initial scribbles to designs with high symbolic content.

The analyst also generously shares with the reader the questions that arose during therapy about her capacity to understand, love, and contain her little patient.

As is easy to see, I have given a brief introduction to the chapters to promote an interest in reading this exciting book. I insist again that it will be of interest to those who work in the mental health field with patients of any age. It will increase our "toolbox" for our daily clinical practice, and who knows, maybe more than one therapist will be encouraged to take a child into treatment. I assure you that they will come out of that experience transformed.

Virginia Ungar, MD, Buenos Aires, December 2024

References

Bick, E. (1941). Child Analysis Today, in: Collected Papers of Martha Harris and Esther Bick, section I, vol. 8. Clunie Press, Pertshire, Scotland, 1987.

Klein, M. (1927). Symposium on Child-Analysis, in: The Writings of Melanie Klein, vol. I. Hogarth Press, London, 1975.

Ungar, V. (2022). Fantasy, belief and imagination. Controversies in Child and Adolescent Psychoanalysis, 31: 14–22, Buenos Aires.

Introduction

Ana Belchior Melícias

The creation and subsequent publication of this book are the result of the work of four psychoanalysts who enthusiastically embraced the challenge of sharing diverse experiences from their analytical encounters with four children. This reflects the richness of pluralism, and that is precisely our daily reality. Clinical practice continually confronts us with the complexity of managing the paradoxes that arise from pluralism and differences within the unique setting of the co-construction of the analytic field in meeting the singularity of each child, family, and analyst.

Contemporary psychoanalysis grapples with a critical question that affects its theoretical foundation, the organization of psychoanalytical institutions, and the adopted training models: how do we maintain complexity and coherence while managing the contradictions of pluralism? Two main distinct positions emerge in this debate. One advocates for convergence and integration to present psychoanalysis as a coherent and consistent scientific discipline to society and to meet academic demands. The other cautions that such integration may lead to simplification and fragmentation of psychoanalysis's unique aspects, emphasizing that psychoanalysis must remain at the boundary, engaging continuously with other knowledge domains without reducing itself merely to a therapeutic practice, given its broader scope since Freud.

The theme of pluralism, articulated within the model of complexity and its correlate *working through*, served as our guiding thread (*fil rouge*) in inviting readers to join us in the "psychoanalysarium," where they can witness and enrich themselves with the fertility of contradictions and differences.

Hence, there was no unifying concern across the different chapters, neither theoretically, technically, nor formally. We aim to showcase each analyst, each analytic pair, in their "psychoanalysarium," discovering, creating, experimenting, imagining, thinking, and transforming into a dream-for-two.

The term "psychoanalysarium," invented and created alongside the birth of the book, encapsulates a blend of work, space, time, movement, dream, creativity, *rêverie*, and phantasy. It refers to both the physical analytic room and the mental setting of the analyst, as well as the potential space created by the analytic field and also the aesthetic dynamism of the unfolding analytic process.

DOI: 10.4324/9781003584018-1

The four authors are members of the Portuguese Psychoanalytical Society, of the European Federation of Psychoanalysis, and of the International Psychoanalytical Association (IPA). They are also Child and Adolescent Psychoanalysts by the COCAP (Committee for Children and Adolescent Psychoanalysis of the IPA). They belong to a scientific "siblinghood," grateful to their society for enriching learning experiences and extensive exchanges in their journey to becoming psychoanalysts. Through a desirable exogamic movement, each author expands her knowledge through scientific affinities and fruitful exchanges with other societies, regions, and psychoanalytical cultures. They are also part of a much broader "siblinghood," inheriting a long lineage dating back to Freud, whose genius discovered and invented the work they cherish, grounded in dream/unconscious and infantile psychosexuality.

Child psychoanalysis has significantly impacted the theoretical body of psychoanalysis since its inception, evident from Hans's visit to Freud in 1922, which led to the anticipated collapse of the first topic (topographic model of the mind) and the emergence of the second topic (structural model of the mind). Freud had high hopes for child psychoanalysis and was always concerned with the infantile, both directly and indirectly, demonstrating the crucial importance of this period in psychic architecture. Apart from observing childhood in adult analyses, Freud had clinical contact with a child, Hans, through an adult, his father. He requested his followers to observe their children and bring notes to him, and he himself, through observing a grandchild – Fort-Da – broke and altered the course of his theorization. Anticipating, as in many other issues, Freud also left seminal notes on infant observation, a crucial area at various levels in psychoanalyst training.

Child psychoanalysis, initiated through the mythic Little Hans, was handed over to pioneering women in the psychoanalytic movement. From the anteroom of this genealogy with Eugénie Sokolnicka (1884–1934), Sophie Morgenstern (1875–1940), Hermine von Hug-Hellmuth (1871–1924), and Madeleine Rambert (1900–1979), we reach the main hall where we find Anna Freud (1895–1982) and Melanie Klein (1882–1960). Klein is unanimously considered the true creator and systematizer of child psychoanalysis, through both play technique and conceptual construction of the infant's internal world (object relations theory). Male pioneers in this field include Sándor Ferenczi (1873–1933) and August Aichhorn (1878–1949), who dedicated their work to children and adolescents. We would also highlight the important theoretical contributions of Karl Abraham (1877–1925).

Passing through the ancestral house, we walk hand in hand with the indispensable contributions of Klein, including projective and introjective processes, the crucial discovery of projective identification, the theorization of symbolization processes, the importance of the interior of the maternal body and the epistemophilic instinct. This is followed by the Bionian and Meltzerian links and extensions.

In the latter half of the 20th century, we proceed with post-Kleinian developments, whose marks can be recognized in the different chapters of this book. René Spitz (1887–1974) introduced concepts of hospitalism and anaclitic depression, identifying three organizers of psychic life: smiling at three months, stranger anxiety at eight months, and the structuring function of "no" at two years. John Bowlby (1907–1990) described predictable behaviors of children hospitalized, divided into three phases: protest, despair, and detachment. Donald Woods Winnicott (1896–1971) highlighted the radical importance of the mother's care in the infant's constitution – "There is no such thing as an infant" – and developed the transitional area and phenomena. Wilfred Ruprecht Bion (1897–1979), placing the mother's *rêverie* as a support for the constitution of the child's thinking process, the continent of the contents to be psychically literate, also dealt with the fetal psyche. Esther Bick (1901–1983) created the infant observation method extended to psychoanalyst training and contributed the fundamental concepts of adhesive identification and second skin. Donald Meltzer (1922–2004) developed the central conceptual axis of psychic space organization (including the claustrum, maternal body geography, zonal confusions), also placing aesthetic conflict as a paradigm of psychic development. Frances Tustin (1913–1994) revolutionized the classical understanding of autism and coined the concepts of black hole, shapes, and autistic objects. Margaret Mahler (1897–1985) proposed stages of normal autism evolving into autonomy and object constancy through the developmental stages of separation-individuation. Jacques Lacan (1901–1981) introduced the mirror stage concept in the child's development of subjectivity, also intertwining the original concepts of the real, the symbolic, and the imaginary. Françoise Dolto (1908–1988), in the Lacanian lineage, developed the concept of the unconscious body image and popularized child psychoanalysis, along with Serge Lebovici (1915–2000), who built new psychoanalytic intervention practices in France. Michel Soulé (1922–2012) helped define psychosomatics in psychoanalytic work with infants and children, and together with René Diatkine (1918–1997) gave great impetus to the progress of child psychiatry through the Alfred-Binet Center, both of whom worked to apply psychoanalysis to multidisciplinary teams. Arminda Aberastury (1910–1972), a pioneer of child psychoanalysis in Latin America, completed Klein's theory by introducing the primary genital stage, including the father in the mother–child relationship from early life.

Our gratitude extends to the numerous contemporary authors whose updates and thoughts provide true scientific *rêverie* and guidance through the darkness.

Freudian concepts have deepened and expanded through the main schools of psychoanalysis – Ego Psychology, Self Psychology, Kleinian School, Bionian School, "Middle Group" or Independent Group, and French or Lacanian School – born primarily from two axes: the reformulation centered on the pulsional dialectic between life drive (Eros) and death drive (Thanatos) as well as the continuous transformation of the relationship between Ego and Id throughout Freud's work.

Returning to the historical origin of child psychoanalysis reveals its birth marked by the antagonism between Anna Freud's pedagogically influenced technique and Melanie Klein's analytic technique. This original controversy proved fruitful, compelling resulting theoretical affiliations to investigate and produce knowledge about psychic functioning. All theories and authors seem to accept the existence of a nonintegrated state from which various psychic processes and arrangements contribute to unification. Some authors put more emphasis on the constitutional, others on the environmental, and still others on complementarity.

The connection between the internal and external worlds appears reciprocally correlated and mutually determined, as Freud conceived in his principle of the complementarity nature of psychic functioning (between primary and secondary process as well as pleasure and reality principles). Contemporary authors seem to be increasingly moving in this direction, addressing the analytical object in this incessant back and forth of intersubjectivity and thirdness. Moving beyond a more evolutionary approach from one phase/stage/position to another, there is now a prevailing idea of continuous oscillation in psychic functioning – of the analysand, the analyst, and the analytic pair – between psychotic and nonpsychotic parts of the mind, between nonintegrated states, partial and diffuse schizoid-paranoid positions, integrated and symbolized depressive positions, and ultimately creative states of the mind.

This can be bridged with child psychoanalysis, which has become a border and crossroad territory, a potential and intermediate space, making it a demanding and stimulating field of work: the adult with the child and the "infantile" in the adult; the child-in-the-family and the family-in-the-child (transgenerationality); play, often nonverbal, "verbalizing" in true free association; drawing as a figurative narrative, weaving meanings as a co-construction in the analytic field; the inseparable and current body–mind – the mind in the body and the body in the mind; fantasy enacted in reality and the concrete reality of fantasy; the more structural factors versus the plasticity of simultaneous levels of psychic organization, etc.

We can say that, starting with the adult in Freud, we advanced to the infant in Klein, proceeded to the internal geography of the maternal body with Meltzer, to the child-with-his-mother in Winnicott, and to the mother's *rêverie* as support for the constitution of the child's own thought in Bion. Continuing in that direction, even further back, the study and observation of intrauterine life have become a current object of investigation. We can say that clinical-theoretical development of psychoanalysis has been evolving regressively, that is, toward the originary, primordial, the early, the archaic, as if we all knew since Freud and through him that childhood/the infantile, just like dreams, is the "royal road." Or, as João dos Santos would say, "the secret of Man is his own childhood."

Paradoxically, and contradicting the evidence of this theoretical-clinical trajectory, child psychoanalysis has been an area with ambivalent contours in the general training of analysts, as if "true" psychoanalysis flourished with and for adults. Are we still trapped in the original Freudian thought, without integrating the enrichment of the hypotheses he launched, developed by subsequent psychoanalytic thinkers? Will there be resistance to the more primitive functioning of the mind, from which we try to separate ourselves evolutionarily? Is it the difficulty in containing the infantile world, fragmented, diffuse, a Mœbian spiral, neither inside nor outside, that our mind struggles to objectify?

Regarding contemporary debates, some authors consider that child psychoanalysis is described by the abundance of its practice – more or less rigorous – contrasting with the rarity of scientific works. Perhaps this is because child psychoanalysis is often confused with the applications of psychoanalysis to children, in psychoanalytic-inspired psychotherapies, mother–infant psychotherapies, family therapies, the use of psychoanalytic discoveries in child education and pedagogy, in analytical psychodrama, as well as in understanding institutional conflicts, among others. All these applications have ended up generating some confusion and distancing child psychoanalysis from the field of psychoanalytic research and the training of psychoanalysts. This can undoubtedly become disastrous, as we know how much of the theoretical body of psychoanalysis has developed precisely through the clinic of child psychoanalysis.

Someone said that without psychoanalysis, today's psychiatry and psychology would be tedium. If, on one hand, psychoanalysis is a privileged instrument for seeking answers to the concrete needs of psychiatry and psychology; on the other hand, it risks distancing itself from what characterizes it as a science, being a research space for internal psychic conflicts through the analytical transference movements in the field. We cannot diffusely dilute the work of the child psychoanalyst, distancing it from the specificity of its laborious know-how, but we also cannot stiffen processes and frameworks into a circular rigidity, without gaps or cracks, where newness and difference can emerge. Consequently, we find ourselves at the intersection between the external demand for answers and the psychoanalytic theoretical-clinical body proper. After all, the status of psychoanalysis seems to continue to define itself as a transitional – and potential – space that needs to be dynamically and negatively (de)constructed in the perpetual movement that generates its true unfolding.

We hope that the "psychoanalysarium" presented here, where the whole is clearly greater than the sum of its parts, becomes a gratifying and fruitful read, promoting new reflections. For us, its elaboration and writing have updated the aesthetic conflict, highlighting the beauty and mystery of the pluridimensionality of the process of two minds interacting in child psychoanalysis, as well as the originality of each analytic process.

Chapter 1

The girl from the sea

The transformation of illusion into development

Isabel Quinta da Costa

Rita is a pretty, delicate girl with a sad expression and a well-groomed appearance. She is accompanied by her grandmother, whose extravagant and overly familiar behavior immediately catches my attention, complemented by a style of dressing that resembles that of a bold and daring teenager.

With an inappropriate attitude, referring to her granddaughter, she begins by telling me, "We are very close friends and understand each other very well! R., tell her why you wanted to come." The girl seems embarrassed, lowers her gaze, and keeps tugging at her shirt as if trying to hide. She timidly says, "I asked for this appointment because I think I need . . ." The grandmother urges her to speak, and the girl, submissive to her grandmother, says, "My parents wouldn't decide."

I attempt to clarify the meaning of these words and realize that the appointment was made without the parents' knowledge. I explain that I cannot conduct the consultation without their permission and presence, but the grandmother becomes irritated and protests uncontrollably, using her granddaughter's struggles to harshly criticize her daughter and son-in-law. The girl becomes uneasy, cries, and defends them, and I try to calm her down by telling her that she was brave to ask for help and that I would see her again if her parents agreed and accompanied her.

Supported by a countertransference feeling, the need to establish boundaries and the obligation to inform and hold the parents accountable for the intervention immediately became evident.

In the days that followed, the grandmother persistently called, asking for an appointment. She even appeared at the clinic without any scheduled appointment because she wanted to talk to me about her daughter. I did not see her in consultation, but over the phone, I insisted on the need to speak with the girl's parents, so she wouldn't remain in that uncomfortable situation, which did not appear to trouble the grandmother at all.

During this time, I felt uneasy whenever I thought about R.

A week later, the mother scheduled an appointment because she wanted to explain everything. She is a young, pretty, and well-groomed woman, very anxious and insecure, who blames herself for what has happened. Filled with a sense of failure in her role as a mother and educator, she is particularly concerned about what I might think of her.

DOI: 10.4324/9781003584018-2

She attributes all that has happened to her mother's behavior and accuses her: "She makes everyone's life miserable; when I was a student, I ran away from home for a few days because I couldn't take it anymore. She ruined my father's life and managed to drive him away from his daughters; she is disturbed! She criticizes me, interferes in my life, and questions how I raise my children. She criticizes my husband. She is unbearable! My sister doesn't allow her in her house anymore, but I can't! I need help, and so does R., she doesn't focus on or care about school; I constantly must stay on top of her, she is very dependent and now has conflicts with her younger siblings. Home is a nightmare, and I feel lost."

Throughout the consultation, I noticed a confusing intergenerational hierarchy, and as I listened to the mother, I heard the voice of a desperate girl, unable to separate herself from a highly intrusive, demeaning, and controlling mother. I was left with the impression of a family of siblings competing with one another, lacking boundaries or clear generational distinctions.

Although I insisted on seeing the father, who was away for work and, according to the mother, didn't have the time, I scheduled an appointment without further delay, since the girl had been asking to see me.

R. came accompanied by her mother and seemed a bit constrained. I started by saying, "Today we'll be able to talk about what's bothering you."

The mother, with a harsh tone and a certain emotional distance, mentioned her daughter's difficulties and disinterest in school, criticizing her for having sought me out with her grandmother without her parents' permission. While listening to her mother, the girl groaned, adjusted her braces, and justified, "It was put on this week, and it hurts a lot. In fact, that's the only reason I'm sad today!"

Finally, alone, she spoke to me again about her braces, the pain they caused, and her difficulty in talking.

A: I know it's hard to talk about anger and sadness, but now, whatever you say stays between us.
R: Is that why you didn't call my parents?
A: I didn't call because I didn't know them, but I never reveal what happens here.

She looked at me with distrust and, in silence, showed me a small notebook with various drawings she had done.

A: Here you can also draw; it's a way of talking.

While she drew various lines on a sheet, she told me she was drawing her braces and opened her mouth so I could see them better. She described each part in detail, its purpose, and especially the discomfort it caused:

R: My teeth didn't have room and were growing crooked.
A: Growing up is hard, and sometimes it hurts.

In response, she opened her mouth again and added:

R: This little metal piece is for straightening – it hurts!
A: To grow up, you need to follow a lot of rules; you need to do everything right.

From a symbolic perspective, as in a dream, the braces seemed to encapsulate her entire problem, and as I listened, I felt that R. was allowing me a glimpse into her inner reality, filled with anxieties and a sense of self that imprisoned her. Without an emotional space that was liberating and reassuring, she felt that, like her teeth, she was growing "crooked" and needed a "little metal piece" to help her straighten out.
 Abruptly, she stopped drawing and said:

R: This one isn't turning out well, I'll make another one.

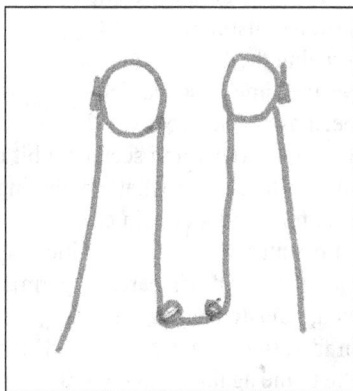

Figure 1.1

She pulled out another sheet from her notebook and started drawing

R: Now this is a chameleon.

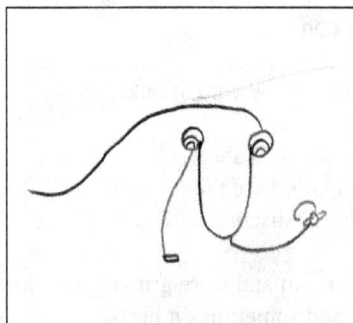

Figure 1.2

Surprised by this change, I asked:

A: What do chameleons do?
R: Don't you know? Chameleons disguise themselves . . . to protect themselves from enemies.
A: Sometimes people disguise themselves too.
R: What? (she laughed) Do you know people who change color?
A: They don't change color, but some people do disguise themselves . . . and you don't know me yet; you don't know if I'm disguising myself or if you can trust me.

She looked at me attentively and stayed silent; then she started making a paper fortune-teller, folding and opening it.

R: Let's see if you can guess . . . Don't you know? It's called a 'fortune-teller' . . . I write things, open and close it, count the numbers, and we find out what happens.

She showed me the inside of the fortune-teller where various names, numbers, and emotions were written, and we began to play.

A: I guess . . . you have friends, you want to discover new things, and you feel anger, happiness, sadness, fear, jealousy . . . (she interrupted me)
R: I didn't write jealousy . . . I never felt that! And I. and T. aren't friends; they're my siblings.
A: Well, sometimes siblings feel jealousy toward each other.

The session ended, and I called the mother back in. She entered anxiously, wanting to know if everything had gone well, asking a lot of questions without waiting for answers – both to her daughter and me. I tried to reassure her and clarified that we would talk again, this time with the father present, so I could learn more about the girl's life story and find, together, a way to understand and help her grow. Reluctantly, she accepted my suggestion, and on the same day, the father called, and we arranged a nearby date without difficulty.

In the interview with the parents, the mother seemed very anxious and tense, and without making any reference to her daughter, she resumed her bitter complaints about her mother, repeating what she had said during the first meeting. The father, who had a pleasant appearance and friendly demeanor, although he shared a similar opinion about his mother-in-law, did not dwell on the subject. Instead, he said,

What concerns me is the way she manipulates R. . . . . We both have difficult mothers and the same profession. My wife was a brilliant student, while I was always weak; I had issues with my mother, who was very demanding, to the point that I developed asthma at the age of nine. The tension at home was enormous, and my father saved me by sending me to boarding school. But even today, I feel the effects – I tend to get depressed, and it's hard for me to make decisions. I don't want the same to happen to my daughter; she has had a complicated start in life.

The mother, feeling her husband's words as an accusation, defended herself and disagreed. However, he calmly explained, "When R. was born, my father passed away, and shortly after, my mother was diagnosed with a terminal illness. I was very depressed, distant, and offered little support at home, and my wife was left alone."

As she listened to her husband, feeling understood, the mother became less tense but very emotional. She began to talk about herself:

I had postpartum depression that lasted several months; my mother was no help, and my husband was barely there. It's true – I felt very alone and helpless then. It was a very critical time . . . I don't even know how we stayed together after everything.

Together, the parents gradually recalled R."s personal history together. The pregnancy and birth had no complications, but breastfeeding was difficult from the beginning, leaving the mother to feel like a failure. During the first months of life, both grandmothers competed fiercely to care for their granddaughter. To avoid this confrontation, the parents decided to put R. in full-time daycare. Two months later, on the pediatrician's advice – and because the girl frequently fell ill – she returned home under the care of a nanny. However, daily interference from the grandmothers, particularly the maternal grandmother, led to strong arguments between her and her daughter that persist to this day.

Meanwhile, the paternal grandmother eventually passed away. Feeling "exhausted," the father consulted a psychiatrist and was prescribed antidepressants, which he still occasionally uses. Unable to support his wife or set boundaries with his mother-in-law, he found a pretext to be away frequently at work.

When R. was three years old, and her brother was born, she started preschool. She showed great difficulties in the separation/individuation process, marked dependence on her mother, and little interest in playing with other children.

At six years old, starting school and adapting to new demands revealed a series of behaviors that had previously been dismissed by her parents. At school, R. frequently cried, showed little motivation for learning, and often clashed with her classmates, leading to repeated feelings of exclusion from the group.

Her grandmother, a retired teacher, frequently went to the school without the parents' knowledge. She criticized the teaching methods of R.'s teacher, blaming her for her granddaughter's lack of success.

At seven, with the birth of her second brother, psychosomatic symptoms began to appear, coinciding with school evaluation periods and often forcing R. to stay at home.

Her teacher expressed concern because R. was not integrating with the group and was not making academic progress, suggesting a psychological consultation. Although she accepted the suggestion, she rejected the psychologist's guidance, eventually clashing with the teacher and, influenced by her own mother, blamed the teacher for R.'s lack of success and interest. She eventually changed her daughter's school when R. was eight years old.

At the same time, projecting her own desire for autonomy onto her daughter, the mother convinced R. to move to a separate room away from her brothers, to try to resolve the increasing conflicts among the three children. Feeling excluded, R.'s rivalry with her siblings intensified, and she began to experience nighttime anxiety, which prevented her from falling asleep without company.

A year after changing schools, the new teacher's complaints mirrored those of the previous one, and this was when I first met R.

During this initial interview, the parents relived their own painful childhood experiences and connected the events in their individual and shared lives. I tried to reinforce the father's role, who, while "weak," was sensitive and insightful, and to support the mother, who felt very guilty and insecure in raising her children, helping her understand that excessive demands and control could hinder children's autonomy and growth, as she herself had experienced in her own childhood.

The intensifying family conflict, with daily interference and criticism from the grandmother leading to violent arguments, R.'s increasing school struggles, and the parents' awareness of their difficulties, created great anxiety but, at the same time, made them receptive to the therapeutic intervention I proposed.

A few days after the interview with the parents, the grandmother, asserting her rights, appeared at the clinic wanting to be seen as well. She reacted aggressively when I suggested she speak with her daughter and son-in-law and referred the decision about her presence at the consultations back to them.

Meanwhile, we began the sessions. R. seemed very interested, and feeling the focus of attention, talked a lot, was creative, enjoyed drawing, and demonstrated insight in response to my comments. About a month later, surprisingly, before a session, her mother called very agitated, unsure of what to do: "R. doesn't want to go; she says she doesn't like it anymore and doesn't need it." Not understanding what was happening, I suggested she bring her in so we could talk, and when they arrived, they were both upset. While the girl cried and said she didn't want to come in, the mother kept saying, "This girl only brings me problems! Yesterday, we had another argument at home because of her! Now my mother wants to take her to therapy! It's another battle."

I told R., in her mother's presence, that the argument wasn't because of her, that it was an issue between her mother and grandmother that only they could resolve. She seemed to calm down, agreed to come into the office with me, but didn't want to talk or draw and stayed silent, "just resting." She then showed me a book of Calvin and his imaginary friend, Hobbes the tiger. Through several sequences, she showed me how Calvin's mother, when angry, turned into a threatening creature, and his teacher turned into a green monster ready to devour him.

A: It seems like what's happening to you. . . . When your mom and grandma argue, you get scared, thinking it's your fault, and that's why you can't come to therapy.

In agreement, and expecting more help from her father, R. showed me another sequence – the mother yelling, telling Calvin to go take a bath, while he, distressed, held onto his friend tiger's ears, which, like his own, were almost coming off because of the noise . . . while the father passively sat in the living room reading the newspaper.

It became evident that R. didn't want to stop therapy; the therapeutic process had been established from the beginning, and my interpretation had facilitated her progress and strengthened the therapeutic alliance, allowing her to talk to me about her fears and her desire/need for a more supportive father to protect her from the "war" between these two important but sometimes threatening figures.

In response, the father called me to confirm the continuation of therapy and, feeling reinforced in his role, decided to intervene and inform the grandmother that he would be the one bringing his daughter to sessions. In this situation, the mother felt understood and supported by the father, and R. was able to continue her work with me.

A few days later, in another session, R. drew a comic strip and narrated this story:

Figure 1.3

R: Once upon a time, there was a sunflower with drooping petals, feeling sick and feverish, so its mother took it to a butterfly doctor. It stayed in bed taking medicine, feeling sad as it watched the sun outside. It didn't get better! The mother took it to many doctors, but nothing worked. It only got worse! Finally, she took it to a sunflower doctor who gave it an injection and tied it with a strong string so it wouldn't fall. It immediately started to get better, and its petals became beautiful again. Later, the mother also wanted to give it medicine, but it didn't want any – it had already taken some and was better!

R: I thought of drawing it this way . . . did you know I've been to many psychologists? (she looked at the couch at the back of the room and continued) There's also a bed there.

A: Do you think you can get better with me, like the sunflower, and feel happier and safer?

The sunflower doctor speaks a language she can understand; they are of the same kind and can undergo treatment together, now connected by a very strong cord. This reveals a latent conflict with the mother, whom she still cannot oppose directly, but who prevents her from taking medicine from anyone else.

Meanwhile, for several days, the central theme of our sessions was her siblings and her classmates at school, whom she couldn't get along with, leading her to feel disadvantaged and excluded in both situations. School tasks, along with the demands of her teacher, were also experienced as an insurmountable problem.

On one of those days, she arrived particularly angry with her mother because

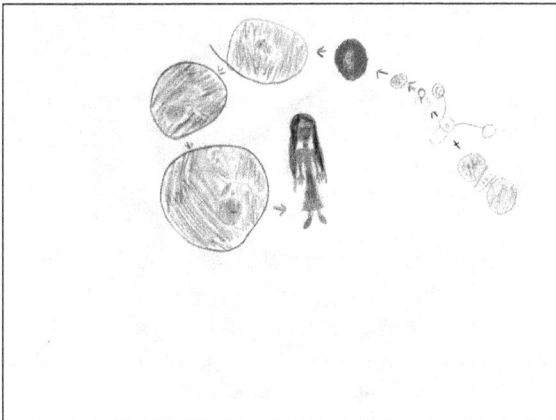

Figure 1.4

R: She always takes my brothers' side.

She took a sheet of paper and started drawing circles of different sizes, filling them with various colors and shapes, and connecting them with arrows.

R: I learned this in school . . . and I don't want to say anything.
A: You're showing me that you already know how parents make babies. (she added another arrow and drew a girl)
R: This is me when I was three years old, before my brothers were born.
A: Back then, all the attention was on you; your parents didn't have other babies yet.
R: Yeah . . . I was the only grandchild, the only niece, the only daughter.

A few days later, she began talking about her house, describing it in great detail, and the "old and precious things" that were there. At the same time, she spoke about her parents' qualities and abilities, and following their example, she drew a floor plan of the house, which became the central theme over nine sessions. In each session, she drew and added a new room, carefully stapling and gluing each one, describing everything in detail. Through this process, she also mapped out various instances and drives developing within her.

R: It's a huge and beautiful house!

But R. lamented that the best rooms, upstairs, were reserved for her parents and siblings. Those rooms are spacious, with large windows and lots of light, unlike hers, which is far away:

R: Three hundred steps down!

And even further separating them, there's a large living room filled with valuable objects inherited from her grandparents. Even the kitchen, fully equipped with the best appliances, has a window facing the garden.
    Finally, at the very bottom, next to the garage,

R: Five more steps down is my room, . . . it has no light, just a tiny window that faces the dogs, who bark nonstop and kept me from sleeping. . . . The room has thick walls, and no one can hear me from upstairs . . . It's next to my dad's studio . . . but at night he goes upstairs, and I'm left alone . . . I chose this room myself . . . Mom says I'm older, so I should have a room to myself.
A: You want to please your mom and act grown up, but you also feel more alone and afraid.
R: I'm not afraid!" (she said angrily). It's just that the dogs bark all night . . . that's why I can't sleep.
A: They're noisy like your brothers.

R: And they smell horrible . . . They poop everywhere!
A: Your brothers?
R: No, the dogs. (she laughed a lot) But you know, when they were born, there were piles of diapers full of poop and pee?! You couldn't even enter the kitchen!
A: So they took over the whole house and your mom's attention, leaving no space for you.

R. took a sheet and added a new space to her room:

R: It's very big, with shelves of books, no window . . . and at night dad goes upstairs.
A: There's a lot of space, but no company, so you feel alone.

The floor plan was not just a representation of the house but also a reflection of the family dynamics, highlighting the power of the parents, who owned a large house filled with valuable objects. Meanwhile, R. felt disadvantaged and excluded, perceiving herself as distant from her siblings – a consequence of her parents' intimacy. Through the drawing, she was able to process her feelings of distance and loneliness. It revealed her ambivalence between the desire to grow up and please her mother and the longing to remain a child and receive exclusive attention.

Shortly after, in another session, she said:

R: Do you know what age I'd like to be? Two years old, so I could sleep in my parents' bed again.
A: That way, you'd be in between them, and they couldn't make more babies.

Figure 1.5

She didn't comment but started drawing a letter and then the sea.

R: Do you know the story of the girl from the sea? The girl was floating in the sea, and a boat appeared, but she didn't care! This girl, when she was three, used to say she was the queen of the world. She was crazy! Then she realized it wasn't true and was very disappointed.

A: It sounds a lot like your story.

R: I've never had any disappointments; when I was three, I was the only child, the only grandchild. I wasn't disappointed!

A: But then your siblings were born.

R: I actually liked it; it wasn't a big disappointment. (she fell silent and spoke again softly) It's just that they were gross! Always in diapers and breastfeeding!

A: And then you felt alone, like the girl from the sea; your mom couldn't stop and look at you.

R: And do you know what? Right after that, the other one was born. It was complete chaos! Just diapers, bottles, a horrible smell of poop!

A: It was a big disappointment . . . so what space was left for you?

R: None; thank goodness I had my grandmother, who gave me presents and sweets and was always with me.

A: She treated you like you were little . . . but you knew you had to grow up.

In one of the following sessions, R. drew a story in squares called "Transformations," through which she expressed her desire to fly, to grow, to transform.

Indeed, changes began to occur, and R. tried to resolve issues without her mother's help and without talking about them at home, whether they were quarrels with her teacher or with classmates. She didn't share her little secrets with her friends. Testing her autonomy, she wanted to do her homework without assistance, even if there were some mistakes, and to organize her school bag her own way.

However, her mother, very rigid and controlling, seemed unable to accept the changes that were becoming evident. And in response to a minor incident at school that the teacher mentioned and of which she was unaware, she accused R. in my presence of lying like her grandmother. She was indignant with me and, in the middle of her criticism, left a threat: "If you keep this up, you won't come to therapy, nor will you have a birthday party."

Feeling devalued and excluded by her daughter's growing autonomy, in rivalry with the analyst, the mother later called me in a very aggressive tone, demanding to know what was going on.

I then proposed another meeting with the parents. In this setting, accusations quickly arose from the mother: the daughter was rebellious, the teacher was useless, and the therapist disappointed her because "she should take care of everything," provide guidance, and share information. And despite R.'s improved academic performance, she hinted at the possibility of replacing the therapist with a tutor.

In a supportive and appreciative tone, I acknowledged the mother's role and tried to make sense of R.'s changing behavior. I clarified to the parents that I did not handle school tasks, leaving that responsibility to them, and focused on maintaining the conditions to continue the therapy.

The father, who was perceptive, emphasized his daughter's progress but was also sensitive and affectionate toward his wife, offering to support her more in the challenging task of raising three children and suggesting they both visit the school together, something that had not happened until then.

This intervention by the father, who was increasingly present and active in the family, seemed to play a regulatory role in the conflict that had emerged and allowed the therapeutic process to continue.

Sometime later, R. expressed fear about her distant bedroom, where no one could hear her, and voiced a desire to be closer to her siblings and parents. As she didn't dare to speak about it with her mother, who would be "furious," she started dragging her duvet upstairs at night to sleep in her siblings' room.

Her mother called me. "What's going on? What should I do? Now she wants to go back to being with her siblings." She requested another meeting, but this time, I suggested she talk to her daughter first to understand what was happening.

During a session around this time, R. spoke at length about "a little cousin, Bibi, who is neglected and mistreated by her parents." She then told me she had spoken to her parents about changing rooms but wasn't sure what would happen, as her mother "doesn't want any changes and always convinces Dad."

A few days later, as if sharing a secret, she said:

R: I'll tell you something. . . . I have a terrible rival. Marta is awful; she wants everything, complains, annoyed me, and I slapped her.
A: You're also irritated with your mom's complaints.
R: That's not it at all!

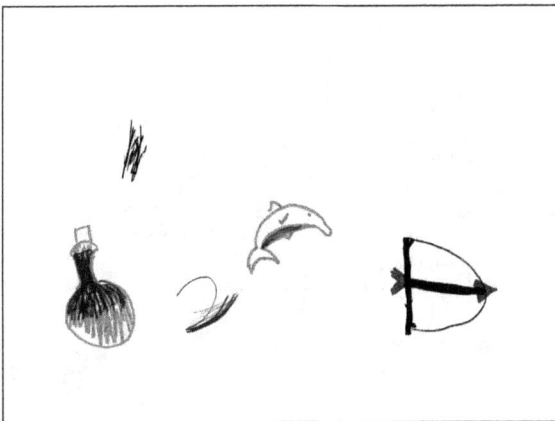

Figure 1.6

She moved away, angry, and grabbed two sheets of paper. On the first, she drew a dolphin, a bottle, and an arrow.

R: They're from a story, but I don't remember it.

On the second, she drew a girl and a boy with a scarf, both without heads.

Figure 1.7

R: The girl's scarf flew away; it's very windy.
A: But they don't have heads!
R: THAT'S HOW IT IS! she said irritably, drawing circles to emphasize it.
A: The girl must be cold.
R: Of course . . . she's running.
A: Is she running away?

She returned to the first sheet and filled in the bottle.

R: It's a remedy that cures everything.
A: What would the girl need to be cured?
R: She didn't know.
A: Without a head, she couldn't think.
R: THAT'S EXACTLY IT. (she shouted)

I understood that R. was telling me about her inability to think, to see her parents together, and to accept their intimate relationship. Feeling excluded and abandoned, like her cousin Bibi, she "runs away, feeling cold." She also hinted at her mother, whom she saw as controlling and "stinky," someone who had everything and prevented her from freely accessing her father. That's why she wished for a magic remedy that would cure everything!

A few days later, she arrived very anxious and agitated, talking about the preparation for end-of-year exams. She didn't sit down to talk, coughed a lot, and said she had been sick and went to the doctor.

R: He told me I was nervous.
A: And do you think so too?
R: Sometimes I'm nervous, and my stomach hurts, or I get asthma.
A: Do you know why you're nervous?

She didn't answer and started drawing, sketching several lines that turned into the face and hair of a green girl.

Figure 1.8

A: Is this the head that was missing from the girl?
R: Don't come up with your questions.

She coughed even more and asked for water.

Then, referring to the current situation in the country, she imitated the voice and manner of an adult and said:

R: The news is terrible; there's nothing but gunshots and arguments, and politicians can't agree. The country is just a mess . . . honestly, there's no solution.
A: Inside you, too, there are conflicts and arguments you can't think about, and they make you feel bad. I think that's why your body gets sick.

She moved away and found the drawing from the previous session (Figure 1.7 – children without heads), bringing it closer.

R: This head belongs to the girl. (she paused)
A: Now we can think about those conflicts together.

She fell silent and seemed calmer.

R: I visited a school; it's big, with older boys, that's where the exams are, with new teachers.
A: Then that must be why you're nervous.
R: Yes, it's a big responsibility, and my mom keeps saying things that upset me!
A: Like giving you bad news, just like on the news.

She then told me about the Brazilian bracelets and the wishes they can fulfill.

R: Just make a wish, and it's always granted by the Lord of Bonfim!
A: You'd like some magic that could fix everything for you.
R: That's exactly it! I'm really worried, but now I study more, and I understand things better.
A: I noticed your cough has improved.
R: But I didn't take any medicine.
A: But you thought and talked about what bothers you, and that brings relief, helps you feel better.

Some days passed, and R. arrived excited; the exams were over, they went well, the end-of-year party was coming up, and the new school no longer seemed so intimidating.

R: Soon the holidays will start, and I'm going to the farm for a few days with my dad. He wants me to help him.

When I told her about my upcoming vacation, R. didn't comment but distanced herself. Shortly after, she looked for paper, glue, and a stapler. She drew, cut, folded, stapled, and glued small pieces of paper, forming a cradle. She added a baby and then a small blanket. Everything was done in detail, as she said she was very good at drawing cradles.

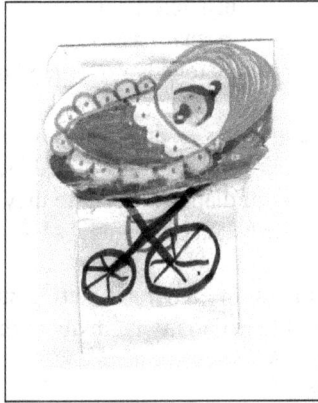

Figure 1.9

She spoke again about her little cousin Bibi, whose parents didn't care for her and even abandoned her.

A: We'll be apart during the holidays, but we'll see each other again. And you know that separation isn't the same as abandonment.
R: I'M TALKING ABOUT MY COUSIN! She yelled and began drawing a lady holding a girl.

Figure 1.10

A: Is that us?

She laughed a lot, cut the drawing into the shape of a photo, wrote "from R." on the back, and placed it on my desk.

A: There's a little part of you, just like Bibi, that needed to be held, but now there's another part, grown up, that passes difficult tests and even helps her dad. Is the picture for us to stay together over the holidays?

She came closer, looked me in the eyes, and gently patted my hair. She picked up the previous drawing (the cradle) and carefully added lace, a pacifier for the baby, and a canopy, along with a bag of diapers, "because they might be needed."
In the following session, she began by saying,

R: I went to adjust my braces; my teeth are getting straighter. I was brave and endured the pain. Then I talked to my mom about the bedroom.

Then, indignantly, she added,

R: I think my mom's a bit silly. Imagine, she made a contract . . . WRITTEN . . . can you believe it? It's for me to promise never to argue with my siblings again. We're getting along better now, but never argue again. Do you think that's possible? I had to sign it, but I signed it with a dull pencil . . . you can barely read it!

Meanwhile, the long-desired bedroom changes finally happened! The parents agreed, the siblings liked the idea, and R., feeling more strengthened and secure, began the climb up the "three hundred steps" that separated her from her parents and siblings.
In the last session before the holidays, R. drew the floor plan of her new room and described it with enthusiasm. It has large windows, lots of light, her bed and her siblings' beds, allowing them to chat before sleeping, and many drawers to store everything.
Almost at the end of the session, she said:

R: Did I tell you I had a very tiny kitten named Mimi? She didn't like being alone; she meowed a lot.
A: Now you're no longer as little as Mimi . . . you're older and stronger.

She agreed and added proudly,

R: Yes, I'm more grown up now; last year's clothes don't even fit me!

Four weeks passed, and R. returned from vacation, sharing with excitement that she had played a lot with her cousins and discovered that her siblings were fun.

R: It was the best vacation of my life; no fights! My dad went abroad, to Asia, and brought back a gift I never would've guessed! He brought a new incubator!

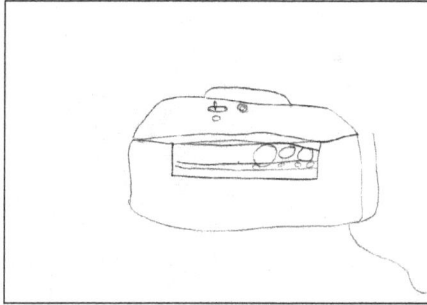

Figure 1.11

While she drew the incubator, she described in detail the levels of shelves, the different bird eggs, and the temperature and light needed for them to grow.

R: It's made of a special, very rare material; here, all the eggs grow very well . . . but you have to be very careful.
R: But you know what happened? Over the holidays, the maid unplugged it! They almost died, weak! It took a lot of time and care to make them strong again.
A: But here we don't unplug anything; we stay connected, thinking together. And you don't seem weak at all!

I understood the incubator as a metaphor for the therapeutic relationship and a symbol of the body in transformation. It marked the beginning of her identification with the analyst, who, with her "special material," was helping her to think and grow. R. seemed to feel, "I'm like you; I have something inside me, something fertile that I can sense and draw but can't yet fully express."

A few days later, still referring to the holidays and discoveries made at the farm, R. told me mysteriously that she had heard about "some strange things" but didn't want to say more. In silence, she drew two circles, added a third, outlined the interior of the first two, and wanted me to guess.

Figure 1.12

A: They look like two big ears, to hear everything.

R. laughed, added eyes and a mouth, and said:

R: It's a smart mouse!

After a brief silence, during which she seemed restless, she continued:

R: At the farm, I saw many animals; I saw a calf being born. I was anxious and disgusted . . . the cow was mooing . . . there was blood and a mess . . . I also saw other things that the dogs do . . . that . . . babies . . . I knew how they were made . . . the parents would go to bed at night, kiss, pass some seeds from one to the other, the mom took a pregnancy test and was pregnant. Now I'm not so sure . . . at the farm, they told me it was like the dogs . . . but I think that's impossible!

As she spoke, she drew a girl and said:

R: She's friends with the smart mouse, and she's wearing a cap to cover . . . don't tell my mom . . . I don't even know what could happen!
A: I hear everything, like the mouse, but I don't tell anyone, so here you don't need to cover your thoughts.
R: They're trembling! (referring to the lines she drew on the girl's legs)
A: Maybe she's scared, like you, with the things she discovered. (she quickly added the missing hands to the drawing, and I continued) And with hands so big, she can also discover new things about her body.

Through her drawing and the accompanying fantasies, R. used the time and space of the sessions to process her psychosexuality.

In the meantime, the school year began, and the transition from elementary to secondary school was marked by anxiety and attention-seeking behaviors, along with somatic symptoms. However, her parents, now more confident and support-ive, understood her struggles but didn't fuel them, maintaining a close emotional support.

Gradually, R. began to integrate and started to enjoy school. She felt safe in class, understood, and took an interest in her new subjects, studying diligently and achieving results that made her mother proud.

At the same time, and often revisiting her holiday memories, she expressed a desire to "try new experiences." So, over several sessions, she began using materi-als different from the usual ones: liquid glue, which she spread on her hands, pencil shavings, paints, leaves, and straw she brought from the farm, which she mashed and mixed with great pleasure and excitement.

When the "mess was too much," she became anxious, interrupted herself, went to the bathroom, and washed her hands thoroughly, with several layers of soap, "because if my mom finds out, she won't like it at all." This revealed a clear

Figure 1.13

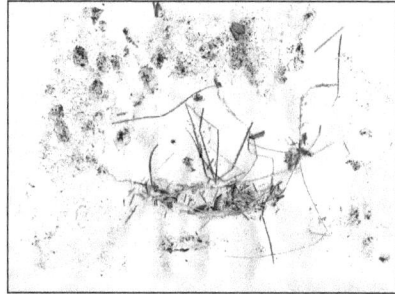

Figure 1.14

excitement of drive-related origin, heightened by sensory stimuli experienced during the holidays. Through the sessions, these experiences could be reflected upon, processed, and gradually integrated into the inner self, enabling greater internal cohesion.

During this time, her mother scheduled a meeting, worried about some new cleanliness habits that R. was showing. I reassured her that these were likely transient and emphasized the need for greater tolerance to help her daughter grow and confront the bodily changes that lay ahead.

I also used this meeting with the mother to remind her of the need for information about menstruation, without frightening explanations, but by valuing this event as an essential growth factor. Denying the evident bodily changes in her daughter, the mother said: "Already?! Isn't it only at fifteen?" She then recounted, still feeling resentful toward her mother, her own experience at fifteen, haunted by "terrifying explanations and guilt-inducing warnings." Afraid to broach the topic with her daughter, she asked me for some suggestions.

Fifteen months after starting therapy, the parents informed me that, due to one of them losing their job, they would only be able to support the sessions until the end of the month. With understanding, I valued R.'s progress, as well as the changes in family relationships, and tried to delay the end of therapy, proposing a reduction in weekly sessions and spreading the payments over several months.

The parents, showing flexibility, accepted my proposal to extend therapy until the Carnival holidays, understanding that an abrupt interruption would hinder the resolution of separation anxiety and the mourning process that could prevent the emergence of new symptoms.

In the session following the meeting with her parents, R. appeared visibly sad.

R: I don't feel well, I'm not coming anymore. (she cried a lot) They told me something else that I forgot . . . when I'm furious, I say "darn it" because swearing is bad and dangerous, and I remember death. (she cried again)

A: Maybe you're thinking about us separating. (she continued to cry) Separation is not the same as dying, and besides, we're not ending just yet. You'll continue coming, as agreed with your parents, and you forgot.

Together, we drew a calendar to mark the sessions until Carnival. As she counted, R. seemed to calm down and stopped crying. In silence, she glued several cutouts and asked me to do the same. She stapled them all together, as if by doing so we would remain connected.

In the sessions that followed, depressive and abandonment anxieties emerged, expressed through stories or movies (the owner who abandoned a dog on the street, friends separated by World War II, etc.). Through interpreting and processing these anxieties in the context of transference, R. gradually became more tolerant of separation.

Figure 1.15

Later, a "sign" of change appeared:
The sky is blue, the sun is shining, and the boy can now cross the street – just as R. was crossing through this period of sadness, "taking big steps" in the process of autonomy and growth.
R. was now eleven, and physical changes had started. She was taller, noticed the development of her breasts and pubic hair, and demonstrated a clear narcissistic interest in her body, which she adorned and perfumed. Her long hair received now

attention, and she felt particularly valued when her father, at the right moments, gave her gifts that enhanced her femininity.

At school, she drew closer to and identified with some classmates with whom she shared interests, and a new activity – dance – allowed her to experience and display her growing body.

In the sessions, masturbation, subtly hinted at in her speech but evident in her drawings, appeared alongside the fear of sin, as taught in catechism, and the fear of punishment.

A few days later, the forbidden was the subject of both drawing and speech. She activated a mix of fantasies and conscious concerns related to sexuality and menstruation, a topic of conversation and secrecy among her friends.

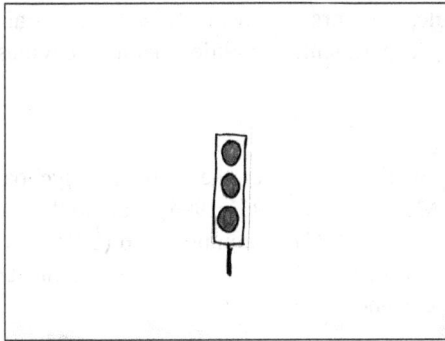

Figure 1.16

Through her drawing, she depicted a sense of imminent danger, represented by a stormy sky in an "upside-down world," swept by "a tornado that strips people of their clothes," leaving them exposed to "the lava of a volcano" that erupted without

Figure 1.17

warning. This drawing seemed to encapsulate, like a dream, all the drive-related conflicts of this preadolescent phase, as well as the stormy and unexpected fears associated with the end of therapy.

However, the progressive internalization of a reliable object and the feeling of being understood enabled her to contain and process her fears, bringing the positive aspects of growing up in the final sessions.

At the end of the treatment, I assured her that I was available for future meetings, and at her parents' suggestion, we scheduled a session for the Easter holidays.

At this point, R. came accompanied by her parents, who shared that they were increasingly capable of resisting her grandmother's demands and had begun sharing responsibilities for their three children. The mother, moving toward greater self-assertion, invested more in her professional activities, which had been somewhat neglected. Meanwhile, R., more confident and secure, was able to advance in the process of autonomy, experimenting abilities that had previously been inhibited.

Note

To conceptualize my work, I drew upon the following psychoanalytic authors: Sigmund Freud (1909), Melanie Klein (1961/1994), Donald W. Winnicott (1977/1987), Arminda Aberastury (1979/1982), Antonino Ferro (2018), Léon Kreisler, Michel Fain and Michel Soulé (1981), Serge Lebovici and René Diatkine (1985), and Simone Decobert and François Sacco (2000).

Chapter 2

Died, slept, dreamed

From immersion in sensoriality to the possibility of thinking

Elsa Couchinho

Throughout Dante's *The Divine Comedy* (Dante, 1304/2013), the character D traverses the various circles of Hell and Purgatory, encountering the punishments of the damned, with each circle differentiated by the nature of the transgressions that determine their eternal fate.

The journey takes place in the company of a poet, Virgil, and when D arrives in heaven, in the company of Beatrice, the primary reason for his quest: the reunion with his beloved.

In Hell and Purgatory, he grapples with doubts concerning the existence of goodness, virtue, and justice, placing his faith under significant scrutiny.

The poet Virgil paves the way, crafting narratives that reflect the plight of the condemned. Yet, a moment inevitably arrives when D must continue his journey unaided.

Beatrice was Dante's first muse. Their initial meeting had a profound aesthetic influence on the young Dante, inspiring his first poem. With her beauty and virtue, Beatrice ignited in the poet a love that was virtuous, elevating him toward the divine.

Writing and the realm of dreams function as spaces where Beatrice's idealized character is constructed, and where contact with her is imagined. Young Beatrice, though destined for an unwanted marriage, died before it could be realized.

Her reappearance in *The Divine Comedy* seems inevitable, restoring the lost object in Heaven, where it might be found once more. The loss of Beatrice appears unresolved, with D seemingly trapped in a longing for reunion. This melancholic state echoes Freud's observation that "the shadow of the object falls upon the ego" (Freud, 1917).

D's reunion with Beatrice becomes a means to transcend his earthly limitations and imperfections, denying his condition, and an effort to reclaim the beloved and lost object. However, in Paradise, amid the arrival of the blessed, accompanied by light and music, D glimpses the possibility of renouncing possession of the beloved object, accepting his human limitations, and his return to Earth. In doing so, he might also accept others in their human frailty.

Flora's case brought this association with Dante Alighieri's work, as I came into contact with her profound psychic suffering (the torments), sadism, and

DOI: 10.4324/9781003584018-3

destructiveness (akin to punishments) that arise from the predominantly pregenital psychic functioning and the intensity of unconscious guilt.

The circles of Hell become the eternal home for the self and its objects, locked in endless repetition, with psychic suffering as their only destination.

Just as D tests his faith and questions his own existence along his journey, so too does the psychoanalyst. In engaging with the patient's psychic reality and the emotional experiences of the therapeutic relationship, the psychoanalyst tests their faith (in the Bionian sense) and challenges their own analytical capacity.

Psychoanalytic theory and the supervisor, akin to the poet Virgil, provide valuable companionship throughout the journey, containing and facilitating transformation and imbuing meaning. They sometimes offer support and protection against the perils of despair, hopelessness, confusion, and acting out. However, the journey ultimately belongs to the individual traveler, who must embrace the possibility of undertaking their path without the tangible presence of the poet, navigating the solitude of their own internal world, replete with its unique representations.

Both the psychoanalyst and the patient must traverse Purgatory and Hell, yet they may also touch upon the celestial – representing the idealization of progress, of their resilience, and of their self-representations and their internal objects, much like goddesses safeguarding blooms (Flora). Nevertheless, human existence unfolds on earth, within the constraints of our finite and imperfect nature, engendering life and processing grief.

The psychoanalytic process we are discussing encompasses the initial three years of a psychoanalysis that commenced when Flora was three and a half years old and ended at the age of eleven.

Flora

The episode that prompted the pediatrician's referral occurred one afternoon in nursery school when F. sat on the floor, facing the wall, repeatedly banging her head against it. She didn't respond to the teacher's voice and appeared detached from external reality.

F. is described by her parents and her teacher as a child prone to significant mood swings: she often becomes angry, experiences inconsolable outbursts without any clear cause, and displays aggression toward her classmates. She is notably uncomfortable with the way others look at her. F. engages with a very limited selection of toys, playing with them obsessively "until she gets tired."

In the year preceding her referral to analysis, F. underwent a neuropsychological assessment, which resulted in a recommendation for a psychomotor structuring program. After two months of intervention, the psychomotor specialist concluded that psychotherapy would be a more appropriate course of action.

Later that year, F. commenced psychoanalytic psychotherapy, with sessions scheduled twice weekly. However, the therapy was interrupted after two and a half months, at the request of her parents, following two sessions where the therapist forgot F., leaving her waiting at the door for approximately ninety minutes.

The journey for F. and her family has been marked by a continuous search for help, beginning when she first entered nursery at the age of two. The various referrals they have encountered appear to be perceived as successive failures, leading to a sense of abandonment, both for F. and her family.

In my mind, I have a representation of a "disheveled," disjointed child, displaying a range of difficulties that seem disconnected from each other.

I reflect on how certain transference-countertransference dynamics may result in negative therapeutic reactions, the abandonment of the therapeutic process, and feelings of fatigue or helplessness, which can lead to the therapist disengaging from both the patient and the treatment.

During my interview with F.'s parents, I am met with their palpable anger toward the previous therapist and their refusal to resume that particular therapeutic process. At the conclusion of our meeting, I discuss the difficulties that sometimes arise in a therapeutic process and suggest that, before my own assessment, it might be beneficial for them to speak again with F.'s therapist, as well as F. herself, in an effort to break this cycle of fragmented interventions.

As I ask questions to gather the anamnesis, I sense a gradual dissolution of the parents' initial distrust. They begin to share both their own and F.'s challenges, expressing that they only recently came to realize that some of these difficulties have been present for a long time. They had not recognized them earlier, likely due to their limited contact with other children.

We agreed that they would contact me the following week to reflect on our conversation and consider the possibility of beginning a new psychotherapeutic process.

The following week, the parents informed me that they had spoken with F. about either returning to her previous therapist or seeing someone new. F.'s response was: "Then I'll call the doctor to say goodbye and tell him that I'm going to play with Elsa now."

After the observation period, psychoanalysis was offered four times a week, accompanied by bimonthly meetings with the parents.

Working with the family

The initial sessions with the family primarily focused on translating F.'s behaviors, enabling them to acquire a communicative value as expressions of her psychological suffering and needs.

The proposal of a psychoanalytic treatment of a high frequency represented a significant commitment and investment from the analyst, contrasting sharply with previous experiences.

Over time, a trusting relationship developed, centered on creating a space that contained the parents' anxieties and their feelings of powerlessness and restoring their confidence in their parenting abilities.

Both parents connected to their own childhood experiences and reflected on how they had perceived parental shortcomings. Working through these experiences allowed them to gain a deeper understanding of the infantile world and the nuances of each developmental stage of their childhood.

For F., it was essential to recognize this strong alliance between her family and the analyst, particularly as the analyst maintained the parental figures in her own internal world, allowing her to express her anger and frustration without destroying them.

As is well known, one of the most challenging tasks for a child therapist, perhaps for all therapists, is to find a balance in the dynamics of cross-identification with both the child and parents. Often, it is within this cross-dynamic of identification that therapeutic work may falter, leading to the potential for the formation of perverse alliances or an inability to identify and empathize with one of the subjects.

Died

F., whom I encounter in the waiting room, approaches me directly. Her gaze is dark and intense, a mixture of sadness and mystery. There is an apparent liveliness that, as we enter the room, translates into restlessness. I am persistently interrupted by her demands, which emerge as shouted commands.

She meticulously surveys the room, selecting human figures: a father, a mother, and a baby. She indiscriminately takes toys and throws them around the room with great force, exclaiming:

> "The baby wakes up, and the parents are having sex." She shouts angrily: "What is this?!!! Tell me! What is this?!!"

She instructs me to remain silent, to turn my back to her, insisting that I do not look while the fights continue. Then, she commands me to look, revealing F. as "dead," covered in blood from the violent fights between the toys, devoid of any distinction between good and bad. Blood and corpses litter the scene. During these fights, toys are hurled against the walls amid intense screaming.

My acknowledgment of her being "dead" and bloodied prompts a nod from her, as if to say: "Right! That's it!" At this juncture, she finally calms down and accepts the interpretation of the end of the session – or the break between sessions – as us being "dead" to each other, as though the analyst casts her out, expelling her, or as if our play had collapsed, reminiscent of her prior therapist's approach.

From the very first session, I experienced a profound drowsiness that persisted until the conclusion of each session. I speculated that this pervasive sleepiness might stem from the same source that caused F.'s previous therapist to forget their sessions.

This sensation of drowsiness was unlike anything I had encountered before; it engulfed my body, rendering me listless and devoid of vitality. When I closed my eyes, it felt as though sleep overtook me abruptly rather than gradually, and amid F.'s demands, I attempted to imagine what I might dream about if I were to fall asleep. All I could conjure was a dark and oppressive setting, lacking images, narrative, or emotions.

In Eshel's work (2001), there is a poignant description of the psychoanalyst's sleep, which also descends suddenly, akin to an injection: a sleep of darkness devoid of feeling, resembling a hypnotic state and identified as extreme dissociation.

In Eshel's clinical case, the patient Clari brought forth the horror of her nightmares, confronting her with the overwhelming presence of something alien, infusing her world with darkness and unfamiliarity.

Clari experienced a horror without content, akin to a near-death experience, as her familiar world collapsed, stripping away her sense of protection and security. The psychoanalyst's drowsiness represented an extreme form of dissociation, a defense against the horrors that the patient evoked.

In the first four months of analysis, the sessions were entirely dominated by F. At her command, I would sit with my back to her while fights and shouting ensued, or silence reigned, resulting in F. appearing bloodied and often 'dead' when I finally was permitted to turn around.

My attempts at speech were frequently met with vehement interruptions and fury, with rare requests for me to leave her, as though her mind was saturated with her own contents, making my presence overwhelming. I could only exist by focusing on what she allowed, echoing her commands, while any gaze or action outside of her directives provoked immense anger.

Throughout the session, F. dictated my gestures, actions, and speech while commanding my gaze. She often covered her ears and shouted, reducing me to a puppet, meticulously following her orders. I felt entirely controlled, every aspect of my being dictated by her.

This omnipotent control that falls onto the analyst, alongside other defense mechanisms that appeared to boycott analytical work, prompts consideration of how Kleinian theory broadens the understanding of psychotic defense mechanisms beyond mere resistance. They serve as organizers of psychic experience and object relations, acquiring a communicative value.

In those early months, I contemplated my role as a psychoanalyst. What was my purpose there when, in the here and now of the sessions, my own mind was frequently struggling to think. F. became my last patient of those days. By the end of the session, I felt "dead," enveloped in a dreamless sleep, disconnected from my internal objects and devoid of emotions, akin to an emptied breast – a nonbreast – distinct from the absent or frustrating breast.

The psychoanalyst's drowsiness can be interpreted as a reaction to excessive and violent projective identification, the fate of beta elements evacuated from F.'s mind (content) to the analyst's mind (container).

F. and the psychoanalyst "turned their backs" – in other words, dissociated – in response to sensations of danger and the risk of annihilation, confronted with a danger without form or name, a "nameless terror."

The analyst was reduced to an object controlled by F.'s omnipotence, diminished to a mere condition (nonbreast).

Yet, when she turned to face F. again, she assumed the role of a witness, reso-nating with Alice Miller's concept (1997) but from a different perspective: she witnessed the destruction, damage, and annihilation of F.'s psychic suffering.

Ultimately, I believe F. sought a container capable of containing her psychic distress, recognizing it while resisting the powerful defense mechanisms charac-teristic of the schizo-paranoid position. This opened the door for the therapeu-tic process to unfold, with the analyst serving as a receiving screen capable of containing and transforming psychic suffering. However, these initial months were fundamentally about not succumbing; they were a time to ensure the object remained resilient.

Slept

With each session, my drowsiness settled in progressively later, not due to the action of the analytical function of the analyst's mind, but rather as a result of F.'s influence, which illuminated the profound connection between her unconscious and mine by incorporating the moments when we both fell asleep into our sessions.

We can assert that the presence of the analyst, as a witness to psychic distress, and her resilience were soothing, enabling F. to become increasingly more con-tained both within and outside the sessions. The initial tumult, characterized by toys thrown across the room, gradually transformed into quieter interactions on the carpet, with the shouting diminishing over time.

However, the fundamental aspect of these months was the "sleeping" that fol-lowed the "dying." While F. struggled to tolerate my words, she found a certain comfort in my sleepiness. Unlike the analyst, who had yet to discover a transforma-tive space for her own psychic suffering, she found a haven for my drowsiness.

The "sleeping in" was a period that followed her struggles and the witness-ing of her "boo-boos." Together, we would lie down and rest, asleep, in soothing silence.

Gradually, the analyst began to introduce remedies to tend for F.'s wounds. Ini-tially, she observed this care, but over time, she surrendered to it, closing her eyes and expressing the consolation she felt as the analyst cleaned her wounds, disin-fected them, and applied bandages and compresses.

As time passed, I began to be able to name and give a narrative to what had tran-spired; the bruises were perhaps the result of pushes and kicks, while the wounds might have been inflicted by bites and scratches. The terror that enveloped F. finally received a name, and only then did she permit me to witness the conflicts, no longer placing me on my back.

It is not solely the psychoanalyst who explores the patient's psyche; patients also delve into the inner world of their therapists. As the analyst identifies the dan-gers and formulates hypotheses to comprehend the destructive impulses, she seems to gain the ability to represent the analyst's mind as a resilient and transformative container for these contents, a space where their link and the reparative function can thrive.

Patients examine not only how analysts contain and transform the session's contents but also the object relations within the analyst's internal world, particularly focusing on their link with parental objects and the parental couple (combined parents).

F. introduced me to an internal realm inhabited by bad objects, whose attacks threatened to annihilate the self. As Melanie Klein (1946) noted, these bad objects emerge from projections of the destructive aspects of the self and the object, alongside the baby's experiences of frustration and discomfort occurring within the schizoparanoid position – in order to protect the self from the anguish of annihilation.

The analyst's intervention commences as a notation (Bion, 1963), noting the repercussions of the destructive assaults and acknowledging the "dead" F., before progressing toward a reparative movement with the remedies.

With the identification of the destructive attacks (kicks, bites, scratches, etc.), the previously nameless terror that F. endured could now be named, thereby diminishing the invasive impact of persecutory anxiety and facilitating a reorganization of her defenses, resulting in a decrease in mechanisms of evacuation and projective identification.

It is through the interpretation of her own destructiveness linked to feelings of frustration and hatred – essentially through the recognition of bad objects as integral parts of the self – that a new dynamic emerges: while psychic functioning continues to be marked by splittings and projections, the idealized good objects can now be represented in play.

As Klein describes, the initial splittings and projections not only exclude destructive impulses from the self, but they also enable links with idealized good objects that shield the self from the attacks of bad objects. The ability to access the idealized good objects brings a narcissistic gain, allowing for the identification and integration of their good attributes into the self.

While sleepiness may dissipate, the moments of playing the "sleepovers" persist within the sessions. The "joint sleepover" represented a profound intimacy, wherein the analyst was finally able to elaborate on some of the session's content, and she awaited the result of these elaborations with keen curiosity.

A pivotal moment occurred when the analyst disrupted her "nap" by mimicking a rooster's crowing. Upon hearing the sound "cócórócócó," F. smiled for the first time, gazing up with amazement and curiosity.

The rooster's crow emerges from the analyst's childhood associations and seems to signify itself a surge of vitality for both, a vital element that bursts forth amid much destructiveness, Eros in the face of Thanatos. Simultaneously, it introduces a limit to the sleep, a boundary established by the analyst that she would later internalize.

Although control over the analyst's movements remains, the analyst is no longer merely F.'s puppet.

Dreamed

With the onset of awakening, we can then imagine what F. has been dreaming about, thereby sketching new boundaries between dreams, fantasy, and reality.

Initially, she expressed her inability to recall her dreams from when she was "asleep"; however, she later began to dream of princesses and have nightmares involving malevolent witches. These witches would manifest as visual hallucinations at her bedroom window, a phenomenon that "sleepovers" enabled her to transform into dream hypotheses.

This marks a period of stabilization concerning her internal objects and their splittings, represented by princesses (as good objects, beautiful entities possessing infinite wealth) and witches (as bad objects, ugly forces intent on destruction).

The witches invade the idyllic realm of the princesses with their envious assaults, seeking to plunder wealth and obliterate beauty, thereby serving as fundamental characters for understanding and working through destructive impulses.

The princesses inhabit the realm of perfection, allowing for a narcissistic reinforcement of the self and its objects, albeit within a partial matrix (partial objects) defined by idealization and omnipotence.

The analyst observed F. in her slumber, noting her awakening and admiring her jewelry and sparkling princess gowns.

Within the circles of hell reside the wicked and the witches, while the virtuous and beautiful princesses dwell in paradise representing the goodness of the self and its objects, thus facilitating peaceful slumber and dreams of positive encounters with the others.

The analyst often adopts the role of a mirror, reflecting the image of the good and beautiful princess, while also embodying the character who admires and envies her, or the protective companion.

As the "dreams" facilitate the elaboration of destructive attacks and the gradual recognition of envy and destructiveness within the self, further differentiations are constructed: F. and the analyst share a cabin and venture into the forest, where they encounter the "bad guys" pursuing them.

The cabin serves as their safe haven, where the lives of the princesses unfold and to which they can always return after their excursions in the forest. The rhythm and timing of the sessions become internalized, allowing F. to experience weekend separations and holidays breaks with increased tranquility, fostering confidence in their eventual reunions.

In the meantime, the representation of the idealized parental couple emerges: the wizard and the analyst combined have the power to repair the damage, expel the bad, and above all, seem to exist exclusively for her.

These objects, the wizard and the analyst/wizard, show us the need and the possibility that the analytic pair has of a third party, introducing difference and the possibility of recognizing benign links between objects (Money-Kyrle, 1967), opening up the possibility of new identifications and experiences of exclusion.

The forest symbolizes the vast, unknown world surrounding F. – an enigmatic blend of fear and allure that evokes curiosity. It represents Mother Nature, from which life is birthed, and can be explored in tandem with "the poet" or at a safe distance under his watchful gaze, with the hope of eventually exploring it independently of these guardians.

The question arose as to whether F., now aged seven, was ready to embark on her first year of schooling. The dynamics of the epistemophilic instinct, which prompted the princesses to explore and discover the forest, led us to conclude that she was indeed prepared.

F. commenced her educational journey successfully and has continued to thrive (she has since completed higher education), gaining progressive autonomy year by year, alongside a growing pleasure of discovering, thinking, and knowing.

Reflecting on those initial encounters, she transports us to a destructive representation of the primitive scene, where her exclusion equated to annihilation. However, this narrative seems to belong to a circle of hell (Oedipus) distinct from that in which F. and her internal objects find themselves (pre-Oedipus).

We revisit her first proclamation:

"The baby's awake! The parents are dating! What is this?"

We return to the sessions, with the analyst's back turned to her.

It may be prudent to consider that the circle of hell primarily belongs to the baby who awakens alone, rather than to the baby who asserts the need for presence, nourishment, and support.

The awakening baby exists in solitude, born of its own destructiveness and the abandonment of the parental couple, at the mercy of a vengeful, persecutory crowd.

The outcome was not merely a "dead" F. but the annihilation of internal objects unable to withstand the intensity of the hateful assaults.

A "dead" F., for the technicians she encountered and for her analyst at the conclusion of each session, at every separation.

Yet, those who "died" are now "asleep" and "dreamed," transforming painful experiences into thinkable content.

When F. attends school, she creates a princess academy where she assumes the role of the teacher, and the analyst becomes the exemplary student she aspires to be, or a pupil who must confront her limitations and rectify her errors. The analyst also embodies the princess, admired and desired by peers or rejected on the playground.

Through this projection onto the analyst, she finds the limits of herself and the feelings of rejection more bearable, facilitating their transformation and reintegration, which contributes to a gradual de-idealization and a less partial representation of the self and objects.

The analyst and F. evolve into two princesses inhabiting a more stable space – a castle – where other princesses and princes reside, along with the wizard and some teachers who impart lessons in magic.

This magic of thinking and transforming is a process that can be "learned" through the integration in the self of the analyst's analytical function.

Just as the analyst has her wizard, she has a romantic partner with whom she rides in a carriage, leaving behind all others, thereby transforming exclusion and positioning the analyst as the excluded.

The analyst must observe her dresses and jewelry and her prince and witness the carriage driving off toward the horizon, where the lovers flirt, leaving the entire life of the castle suspended until their return. "The baby's awake. The parents are dating. What is this?"

It is a mysterious journey that we can only imagine – a walk for parents that one day children will create for themselves. It is a journey that children may dream of within the safety of a castle, inhabited by their return and the comfort of good company.

Lived

It is not feasible to summarize the entirety of F.'s analysis within this chapter. However, one can discern the transition from precursory elements from *The Divine Comedy* to a "lived" experience rooted in terrestrial conditions, closely aligned with the principle of reality.

In this earthly context, the dynamic between the schizo-paranoid position and the depressive position becomes viable, facilitating a gradual integration of the self and objects, which become progressively less fragmented and idealized.

This condition also allows for the elaboration of pregenital contents, creating a mental space for the emergence of proper oedipal themes, ultimately paving the way for genitality.

F. began to integrate the distinction between external and internal realms as well as between fantasy and reality. Thoughts and emotions gained considerable freedom without the confusion that arises in the absence of such boundaries. These limits and freedom are established within relationships with others, which inherently seek meaning.

It is worth noting that this analysis commenced in conjunction with bimonthly meetings with the family, which, like F.'s sessions, were progressively spaced out.

This decision to conduct such frequent sessions with the parents warrants ongoing reflection from the analyst, particularly regarding the transferential and countertransferential elements that motivate this choice, as well as the dynamics of the identification that arise with the child and the parents.

Regardless of the framework of the sessions with the parents, the child psychoanalyst must be adept at translating the child's world for the parents, making sense of their communications, allowing the child to be conceptualized and felt in a less saturated way within the parents' minds.

F. completed her analysis at the age of eleven. At the time of this publication, she has enjoyed her academic career.

Over the years, she has made several occasional visits. During her initial visit, her desire to ensure the possibility of future returns and her wish to appear older were readily apparent.

As a teenager, she presents as an individual with a profound and brilliant gaze, reflecting on her journey while dreaming of her future. She possesses the remarkable ability to think critically and to consider others in a tolerant and humane manner. Now, as a woman who has completed her higher education abroad and has achieved professional success, she continues to grapple with her relationships with her peers.

Patients depart, toward the horizon, while the analyst remains. As analysts, we can be grateful to the families and children, both inside and outside the analysts, who enable encounters wherein narratives and characters are shared – encounters that humanize us and foster growth, bridging the realms between feeling and thought.

References

Bion, W.R. (1963). Elementos em Psicanálise. Imago, 1991.

Dante, A. (1304). A Divina Comédia. Quetzal, 2013.

Eshel, O. (2001). Whose Sleep Is It, Any Way? Or, "Night Moves". International Journal of Psycho-Analysis, 82(3): 545–562.

Freud, S. (1917). Mourning and Melancholy, in: The Standard Edition of the Complete Psychological Works of Sigmund Freud, vol. XIV (1914–1918): On the History of the Psycho-Analytic Movement, Papers on Metapsychology and other Works, 237–258. The Hogarth Press.

Klein, M. (1946). Notas sobre alguns mecanismos esquizóides, in: Inveja e Gratidão, vol. III das Obras Completas de Melanie Klein. Imago, 1982.

Miller, A. (1997). The essential role of an enlightened witness in society. https://www.alice-miller.com/en/the-essential-role-of-an-enlightened-witness-in-society/

Money-Kyrle, R. (1967). Cognitive Development. International Journal of Psycho-Analysis (49): 1968.

Chapter 3

The ghost of a thousand ghosts

From the hunger of a thousand babies to the progressive possibility of symbolization

Raquel Quelhas Lima

Peter was four years and five months old when I knew him. He lived with his parents and a seven-month-old sister. The mother was a gynecologist and the father an engineer. They came to me by the recommendation of a colleague of the mother whose daughter did psychotherapy with me.

The parents mentioned that P. had a preferential relationship with his father, with whom he often slept and with whom he was very possessive. He was the dominator and aggressive toward his sister and peers and very intolerant to frustration. He was afraid of elevators, of noises, and of the toilet. He also had nightmares and nocturnal enuresis. The parents related the symptoms with the postpartum depression that lasted about two years during which the mother had suicidal ideation that led to the sudden interruption of breastfeeding of P. when he was 8 months old. The mother spoke about this period in a very rational and intellectualized manner, using a scientific language, seeming to me that she was defending herself from underlying painful feelings.

The parents highlighted the frequent discussions between them. Both recognized inconsistent attitudes of the father alternating permissiveness with excessive severity. He tried to compensate the son for the mother's unavailability, but his presence near P. was by working on his computer while P. was watching TV or gaming on another computer. P.'s father got worried when he heard him say to his teacher that he didn't know how to play.

I found P. a cute little boy with a sweet appearance. In the three initial consultations, he tolerated well the little attention we gave him. I noticed that he didn't show any interest on the ludic material. He rarely spoke, but he explored the office with curiosity without exceeding the limits that his parents placed on him.

I stimulated him to draw and to use the toys, but he refused my proposals. His behavior was very regressive, speaking like a baby and rolling around on the floor.

The mother seemed to me very insecure and eager for help but needing to present the opposite image. The father was rather obsessive and rigid but wanting to do his best.

There was a history of depression in both families and of suicide attempts on one side.

DOI: 10.4324/9781003584018-4

The mother's absence and affective disconnection and the father's presence without a real relationship with P. did not allow the interiorization of a good internal object that would make it possible for him to separate and have access to symbolization: he didn't know how to play. Only through a close relationship with him could it be possible to understand his relation with the parents and find a way out of that situation.

At the next appointment, the parents were alarmed. P. had hurt a girl with scissors and almost threw a stone at a boy. He seemed indifferent to the suffering of his colleagues and little aware of the seriousness of his behavior.

The proposal of a psychoanalysis on a frequency of three sessions per week was received by the parents with relief. I appreciate the availability that both parents showed to make the treatment possible, despite having a baby daughter and busy professional lives. Concerning the ways I would include the parents in the treatment, I realized that I had to be cautious, avoiding reinforcing the insecurity they felt regarding their parental abilities, following their demands rather than requesting often their presence.

On the first session, P. came with his mother from whom he separated too easily, being the first time he was alone with me. He started to put together a puzzle and asked me for help but then said I was doing everything wrong.

P: I'm going to call mommy. She's the one who knows.
A: Your mommy knows a lot of things, but perhaps you can discover other ones here with me.

We built the puzzle that forms a track on which circles a small windup truck.

P: I'll get the other truck, and we can play shocks, one against the other.

The way P. used the track to play shocks reflected his need to understand the relationship between his parents – the shocks, the arguments. He was also trying to understand how the relationship with me could be. He lay down with his legs in the air and said, as if looking for limits,

P: I'm not going to do a somersault here.
A: You still don't know what it's like to be with me, if it's like being upside down, different from being with mom.
P: Now I can't use my game; I have to come here.
A: How do you use your game?
P: With a video game controller, how else could it be?! Now I want to go to my mom.

The next session, P. wanted to go to his mother shortly after arriving. I told him he could talk or draw about her instead, but he replied that he didn't know how to do it. I suggested that we play moms and brought a little house with furniture and a family. P. found it "very perfect," but he added that he didn't know how to play with toys. I told him that maybe he could discover new things and come to understand his fears. He said he was afraid that his parents would enter the elevator, and he would be left out. Then he held a pillow above his head and suddenly threw it back into a trash can. He repeated the movement several times. I told him it was as if that pillow were his fears and he wanted to get them out of his head and throw them in the trash. He laughed. He returned to the little house, but when he touched it, a step came loose. He abruptly said he was going to destroy everything, and he left the house completely undone.

P. didn't know how to talk about his mother because he didn't have her inside him. To feel her help, he needed her presence. He was with me but felt alone: there, as inside the elevator, the parents were out. However, this was a place where he could get rid of his fears, throw them in the trash can, a container for his internal garbage. When the step came loose, he needed to reassure himself that, there, he could build and destroy. He was testing me; he was seeing if I got angry.

In the third week, he came for the first time with his father from whom he refused to be separated, crying and begging him not to leave him. The father locked him in the bathroom, and after strong reprimands, he handed me the son that I had to hold firmly. He cried desperately and screamed, clinging to the door handle. I tried to calm him down by saying that I understood that it was difficult for him to leave his father because he felt like he was alone. But in reality, he was going to stay with me, and we were going to be fine. I dried the tears on his face, and I quickly caressed his head. He stopped crying and said,

P: OK.

I proposed that he draw with me, and he accepted. We drew alternately, and the result was a set of scribbles. At the end, P. said that the drawing was a pullover, which surprised me. Then he asked for my pen. I told him I had it in my box. He commented that it was "a very special box."

P. was discovering that the analyst/very special box had powers within her that he was still unaware of but was beginning to imagine capable of containing his fears and anguish, a pullover/psychic envelope offered by the analyst's container function.

At the next session, the father expressed that he was relieved to see that his son came calmly. P. drew his family and included me in the group, at his side.

In another session, he sat down on my chair and exclaimed,

P: Ah . . . It's so soft!
A: You feel good here.
P: Do you sleep here?
A: You want to know if I'm here all the time thinking of you or if I also go home to be with my family.
P: That's exactly what I want to know!

Without waiting for an answer, he lay down on the couch.

P: Ah . . . it's so good!

He got up, went to get a sheet of paper, drew two wheels, and asked me to do the same.

I drew two wheels and made a car. He thought it was a good idea and copied. He asked me to continue, and I drew a trunk. He made another one from which a line came out for the trunk I made. He explained:

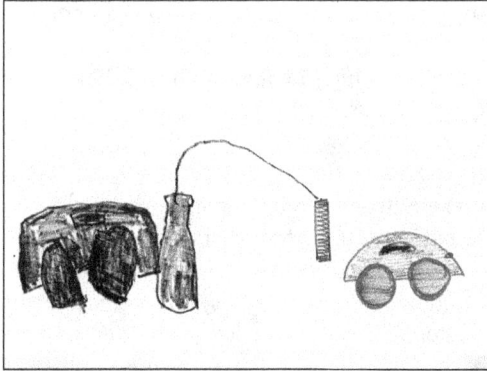

Figure 3.1

P: It's a cola bottle that pours liquid into "this."
A: What's "this"?
P: I don't know.
A: Our drawings are connected as we are connecting too.

The link he made between our drawings symbolized the therapeutic alliance. In the car/body, he highlighted the wheels/the breasts. The liquid passing from one side to another was the milk/psychic nourishment that he was receiving there. The contact with the analyst was that of a relationship with a mother/breast. He was revisiting a very regressive desire for closeness: the intimacy of breastfeeding that he could have witnessed with his sister's birth and that he was unable to completely satisfy.

Over the course of the following sessions, P. would lie on the couch, curl up, stretch, turn front and back, stick his head in the cushions, and sink into them with exclamations of pleasure. The satisfaction he had in the regressive behavior he experienced there was evident. In one session, he asked me to cover him with a blanket, and he rubbed against the padding in autoerotic rhythmic movements playing with his own body and saying: "cushions." Then he lay there without moving.

A: P. fell asleep and is dreaming.
P: Keep going, keep going, don't stop!

A: Once upon a time there was a little boy who wanted a lot a mommy/breast/cushion.

P: Don't stop! Keep going!

A: The little boy lay down on a blanket because he wanted to be a baby again.

He laughed with satisfaction and said he was thirsty, which happened often.

At this stage, he endured separations very badly. He showed a great eagerness for sessions. He expressed cannibalistic fantasies of oral incorporation and of what would exist within the analyst/mother: "Did you know that mother spiders are bigger than father spiders? And do you know that mother spiders eat spider fathers?"

Between two sessions in which I couldn't be with him, he said something that I didn't understand, and furiously, he shouted at me:

P: You never hear what I say! You are deaf! Sit there! Let's talk! I say a word and you guess. These are two words beginning with "s".

A: One word is "thirst": you thirst for coming here. The other is "deaf": as there was no session and I was not here to hear you, you think I became deaf.

P: (laughing) It's nothing like that: it's "key" and "cup."

A: (realizing that, after all, the "s" was "ch" – in Portuguese: "sede" – "surda" – "chave" – "chávena") Here, with me, you will find the key to discover new things that you are thirsty to drink, and for that, you need a cup.

P: (laughing) It's nothing like that.

He went to the couch playing baby and suddenly started throwing everything in the air and screaming:

P: Everything will be messy!

A: As there will be no session again, you want to mess everything up so I can't be here with anyone else.

P. stopped screaming and listened to me. He asked me how much time was left to finish the session. He wanted me to count with him the turns of the hands of the clock until the end.

Over the months, P. tried to deal with the separation by controlling the time watching the clock, turning his body on the floor, making his arms and legs the hands of the clock, or counting the seconds with me.

He also tried to deal with the separation through the game of the "runaway ball" and the game of hide-and-seek, games that he needed to repeat several times:

P: What a naughty ball! Can you see the ball?

A: No. I'll call it: ball!

P: I found the ball! It's here in my hand. But it doesn't come out, it's glued! Look, the ball ran away again! Always on the run! What a runaway ball!

A: Maybe you're afraid that I'll run away from you, like the ball, and you imagine being able to have me always by your side/the ball glued to your hand.

P: Tomorrow there's a party at school and I don't know if I can come here.

A: Maybe tomorrow you can't come, but you'll come next week. As in the game of the ball, we separate from each other, but we meet again in each session.

Two months after the beginning of the analysis, the father called to inform me that P. tied a string around his neck at school, saying that he was going to kill himself. The father blamed himself because he got angry with him the day before. We arranged a session with the parents.

In the session with P., I said to him that his father had told me about what happened at school. He commented: "It was a funny thing, but you must think it's bad."

Then he cut out "a pair of huge pants," as if looking for a paternal figure who would put limits on him. In the following sessions, he directed increasing provocations at me by pulling the curtains, giving orders, making threats, punching the couch and kicking the wall, throwing pillows and pens, scratching the carpet, and at the end of the sessions, refusing to leave.

A: It seems that you want to know who is in charge here, who wears the pants.

P: You do nothing!

A: I do nothing, but I say what to do. I say when there is a session, I say when it starts and when it ends. I am in charge here, and that makes you furious. But instead of talking with me about it, you mess my things up.

He stood still and in silence. Then he began to tidy everything up. He was capable of listening to what I was saying; he was receptive to internalizing.

In the session with the parents, they reported that P. challenged them and, quietly, pushed his sister. At school he was being watched by an employee. The parents wanted me to talk to the teachers because they considered their complaints to be exaggerated. Despite the incidents at school, they felt safer with "this rearguard"/holding that P. materialized in the following session by modeling a cane in plasticine.

The following month, he started playing the "ghost a thousand ghosts," the "ghost thousand babies" that wanted to eat me. He also began to play "the three little lions who lived in a house with a large food store," saying that he was zero years old and was going to turn one, like his sister.

The "ghost a thousand ghosts" represented the hunger of a thousand babies that P. felt. He could have the fantasy that his sister, when breastfeeding, would swallow his mother (would get hold of the food store). The sister was small, but she had their mother all to herself. That's why he pushed her, trying to get her out of the way.

In the session before Christmas holidays, he hid and left a trail made of little pieces of paper so I could find him, as if he needed reassurance that we wouldn't get lost one from the other during that period.

After the holidays, I received the teachers in the presence of the mother. They mentioned P.'s aggressiveness that was moving other children away. However, they noticed a positive change in him. I valued the measures they took to improve the integration of P. in the class. I suggested that the surveillance be discreet so as not to feed his omnipotence. The session seemed to reassure the teachers and, above all, the mother.

In a session that month, P. drew a car with a large wheel at the front and a small one at the back and he, also very small, inside the car.

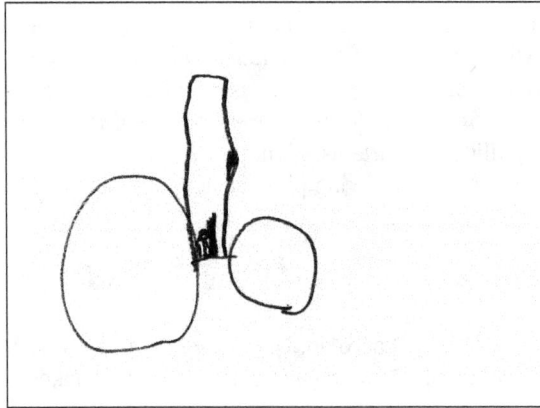

Figure 3.2

Then, he sat at my desk. I reminded him that he couldn't be there. He got furious that I was the one setting the rules. I explained to him that it was natural to be that way once I was the grown-up and the doctor (the way his parents referred to me).

P: My mother is a much better doctor than you! She opens bellies!
A: I'm sure your mother is a very good doctor. Here we don't open bellies, but we open ideas.

P. compared his mother's power with mine. The sadistic fantasy of opening the belly was the fantasy of being able to look inside the analyst/mother's body where he could imagine his father's penis also was. He also wanted to understand his own inside. His father was powerful, he had a big penis (car with a large wheel at the front), while he saw himself with a small penis (small wheel at the back).

The avidity he had for the analyst's riches appeared in the following games. Using cheating, the ghost a thousand ghosts managed to extort money and treasures from me and laughed with delight at so much wealth. He ended by giving me a box of money. Without touching me, he put his hand between my legs and said that

I was shooting laser beams there. I told him he imagined I had a lot of power inside me. So, on the one hand, he took everything from me, and on the other, he gave me alms, lest I get angry with him. On that day, he made a point of leaving "everything very tidy." When he came out, he threw himself to his mother and hugged her, filling her with satisfaction.

P. often said he wanted to poop but was afraid to use the toilet out of his house. One of the times he was talking about poop, he told me he had a lot of money. I told him that when he kept the poop inside him, he felt rich and powerful, like the ghost a thousand ghosts who gets all the money. He replied that he wanted to buy a boat and take everything we had there inside it. We could go together to the sea, with huge and scary waves, with skeletons, vampires, zombies, and devils so that nothing bad could happen to us!

There, with me, P. was feeling able to face the fears he had. The feces were his persecutory interior, the chaotic and aggressive material over which he wanted to have control. He was confounding the feces with the phallus, which made annal the aspects of power and potency symbolized by money. Retaining feces was a way of asserting himself and, simultaneously, of controlling aggressiveness and dealing with the castration anxiety.

The erotic aspects appeared in a session in which P. pretended we were calling his mother.

P: Ask her if my father is home, ask quickly, now!
A: You want to know what your parents are doing together when you're not there.

He kept silent and, subtly, gave me a little kick. Suddenly, he started dancing and singing "Gangnam Style," which he interrupted, embarrassed. I repeated the chorus, and then he started dancing again, shaking his hips while singing "sexy lady."

After a short vacation, he fought with fencing gestures while announcing triumphantly,

P: I cut off your hand! I cut off your other hand! I cut off your head! I cut off your body! I cut off your legs!

During the holidays, P. had felt cut apart, and now, he was the one leaving me in pieces. But he feared the consequences of the agressivity implied in this display: he was needing to go to the bathroom but retained his feces until the end as if, by defecating, he could lose his body's integrity. Defecation was experienced as an anal equivalent of castration anxiety that, at that time, still had a dimension of annihilation.

At the end of the month, he told me that he was going on a snow vacation with his father and brother, feeling his masculine identity reinforced: "Only men go, women don't know how to ski." When he returned, he saw a ball out of place and wanted to know whom it belonged to. He rejected my interpretation of his difficulty in accepting that I could be there with other boys and that he was imagining that I could allow them to do things that I don't allow him to do, such as leave things out of place.

In the next session, he wanted to play with marbles but became furious every time he lost the game. He was cheating, and when I confronted him, he started shooting marbles in all directions. He picked up a pencil made of several interlocking pencil nibs, but he dropped it, and it fell into pieces. He then stopped, worried.

A: You are so angry with me that you imagine that I can get angry too and leave you in pieces, like the pencil.

He listened, silently, and I continued:

A: Maybe you're afraid to poop here because you feel like you're missing out on a part of your body.
P: It's nothing like that.

He started to pick up the marbles, but he collected them with his mouth which became full of balls.

The marbles represented the feces that he sometimes retained, sometimes expelled like bombs in an attack on the mother/analyst.

In the session with the parents, they mentioned that P. now got along better with his sister and that there were no complaints at school. The mother felt particularly happy because her son was now getting along with her so well and with his father too, who, also like him, was now more self-confident, placing more limits on his son. Even so, the father was afraid of the consequences of this new attitude. I emphasized that the limits he imposed were the limits of reality itself and that they were important for P. to grow and relate better with others.

In the sessions, P. continued to make violent attacks on me that demanded readiness and firmness and exhausted me. At the same time, he frequently left his objects in the office (magnets, a ribbon) showing his need to be remembered and his desire to be attached to the analyst, like with a magnet or a ribbon.

In a session, P. wanted to play with marbles but couldn't accept losing. He started throwing them while saying scary things about dead people and zombies. He told me he was out of control. I told him he was scared of what could happen because of that part of him that didn't know how to lose. Suddenly, he wanted to go to the bathroom. It was the first time that happened outside his house during those six months of analysis. He took a long time and returned saying he felt much better.

He was relieved because he had thrown away the filth that he felt he had inside, aspects of himself that he didn't like and that followed him like zombies. Clean, he could be loving with the analyst without destroying her or running the risk of being destroyed.

In the next session, he was furious because I easily found a ball that he hid. He threw it violently at me and hurt me badly. I reprimanded him strongly.

After that, he missed five sessions in a row that I experienced with guilt. In fact, I felt exhausted and had wished, several times, that he wouldn't come. At that time, the containment by the supervision group was of great help. I decided to contact the parents who were embarrassed because they had made a mistake with the date of my vacation.

The following month, P. started playing the bus; he was driving and I was the passenger. I was supposed to move to his place, but I was not allowed to press the red button. He told me in a low voice that I should disobey, and poop would fall on my head. I pretended I washed myself but ended with more poop; I went to the doctor, but he told me to eat poop. After that, P. spent a lot of time taking care of me, cooking for me, feeding me, and bringing me toys to play with.

In previous games, the poop/persecutory interior was used in the relationship with the mother/analyst through retention (omnipotent control) or expulsion (attack). Now, the material was being brought into the game and could thus be elaborated. P. also started using toys – the doctor's bag, pans, plates and cutlery, plushies, and the cars' track.

In the session before my vacation, P.'s game alternated between manifestations of tenderness and attack and kill my plush doll and then save it. I told him that I understand how difficult it is for him not going there. That was making him feel like doing bad things to me, but he didn't want me to be angry with him. After asking me to repeat it, he said: "That's it." When I said goodbye, he regretted that the next session was not the next day. He was beginning to be able to put into words what he felt.

In the following sessions, he maintained games with the plush dolls. Little white men were saving the others from dangerous situations. They had a white barracks and were forming a white army commanded by a white giant.

The splits between black and white, dirty and clean, bad and good appeared in the games, allowing a process of progressive integration:

P: I am the "white man," and you are the "black man". I throw ice and fire through my hands, and you throw shit. The white man always escapes the black man's attacks.

A: You don't want to feel poop inside you so you put it all on me. That way, you can imagine yourself white/clean of dirty ideas.

P: (after listening carefully) Look! The poop fell on me! Now you can also have the power of ice and fire and come to save me.

A: You realize that, sometimes, I tell you things you don't like, but I also calm you down and comfort you.

The game functioned as a transitional object, simultaneously inside and outside him, which allowed him to build a subjective support. He needed to repeat the games and balance his desire for protection with the need to grow. Phallic aspects began to appear in the games and content he brought – the interest in my high heel shoes, tall buildings, and rockets.

On a very hot day, P. asked me to leave the window open. I replied that, in that case, we would have to play "pretend there's a glass window here." He should stop every time I would say "glass." He asked me why we could not go beyond the window. I answered him that our space was on this side of the window, inside that room, just as the place of his thoughts was inside him.

Like in relation to time, P. was experiencing the notion of space. Time and space were abstract notions he could not control or see as "the millions" of the sums that he wanted me to do with him: "How much is a million plus a million?" He was experimenting in an attempt to mentalize these notions, having implicit the fear of being alone – he was preparing himself for separation. He invented games about dying and going to heaven from where one could always be resurrected: we could go to the "first heaven," to the second, the third, and so on, until the "seventh heaven," the "infinity," and the "infinity and beyond," rehearsing the possibility of surviving the separation of the upcoming summer holidays that he was experiencing as having a risk of death.

Before this interruption, he played a guessing game with me. He drew two ants and asked,

Figure 3.3

P: Can the red ant kill the other?
A: It can!
P: Good! You got it right! You're good at this!

Figure 3.4

Then he drew "a walking cactus and a man" and asked,

P: Can the cactus kill the man?
A: No.
P: Right!

P. attributed me the power to guess and was trying to be sure I had all that wisdom that makes him miss me.

He drew a row of circles that he said were lights and made doodles that he explained were "static electricity."

He continued the riddles:

P: Do you know what it is?
A: There are lights to see better and electricity to give energy.

He made a black ball and continued:

P: And that?
A: A black hole.
P: You got it right! Th't's it!
A: Today you feel like a red ant, capable of killing me. You imagine that while we are apart, I can go for a walk with a man and forget about you. You are afraid that the lights here will go out and you will feel sad and alone, like a black hole.

He stood still, listening. Then he made some scribbles at the top of the sheet and asked,

P: Will the universe kill it all? Yes, or no?
A: As if our separation were the end of the world.

Furious, he crossed out the paper, tore it up, and threw it in the trash. I took the drawing and told him:

A: I will paste your drawing and keep it, the same way I keep you inside me. We can remember each other during the holidays, and that can be our static electricity.
P: Okay. You can keep it here, but don't talk about it anymore.

When, a month after, we resumed the analysis, P. placed his hand on my arm and remained concentrated for some time. Then he looked at me and said:

P: I was checking to see if there was static electricity.
A: If I haven't forgot you.

That week, P. arrived furious at a session because his mother did not tell him about a conversation she had had with his father. In the next session, he simulated a fight between himself and the "bad guys" who were attacking him in different ways but from whom he defended himself with numerous tricks. Then he began to sing a song about a boy who was lost and wanted to go home.

A: Maybe you also felt lost without this house. You had to fight alone against the "bad guys"/the things that ail you – staying out of your parents' conversations, out of the time I spend with my family.

With the beginning of classes, P. began to have a growing interest in writing numbers and doing math. The time counts, that we often did, began to be accompanied by written records.

A: It's hard to understand time – you can't see it; you can't control it. Even counting and writing, neither you nor I can prevent time from passing.

In other sessions, we played "powers": power of fire or ice, of electricity or shock, of light or skulls, opposite powers that canceled each other out in attacks. Sometimes he fainted and said that I should go and treat him, sometimes I was the one who fainted, and he came to help me.

After a year of analysis, the grandmother told me that P. had won the award for best behaved at school that week. On that day, we played "little monsters": to evolve and pass the level, we had to eat, drink, and sleep. P. ended up lying down, relaxed, and told me to rest too. I interpreted it as the difficulty of growing up but how he was discovering that it could bring him satisfaction/prizes at school.

In the session with the parents, both mentioned the compliments that P. was receiving from the teacher. At home, he had stopped having nightmares, was sleeping alone, and had no enuresis. The mother recalled how P. rejected her before starting the analysis and rejoiced at how they now got along so well. She acknowledged that she had been estranged from her son and that they had not always had harmony between the couple, perhaps because, before, she was not able to impose herself except aggressively. The father valued my intervention, which he considered "scientific." Both felt it was important to be supported in the exercise of authority.

In a session of that month, P. wanted to be a good little monster, "puppy type," and wanted me to be a bad little monster, "red toad-horse type." I had the "power of milk, the power of food, and the power of sleep" and explained:

P: The milk power was to give poisoned milk to my enemies who would die; the power to eat was to give them food with a magic potion that would take away their powers; the power to sleep was to give nightmares to my enemies who would think that was really happening.

After the explanation, he began to walk like a sleepwalker and said,

P: Your enemies would walk like this, with nightmares of spiders, huge spiders that attacked them and came on top of them. They were thinking about what was happening to them and screaming in fear. They could also have nightmares of suricanes that are balls with spikes all around, balls that we can throw and destroy our enemies.

He was hesitant because he did not know if he should throw the suricanes with a gun or with the hand. With your hand, you could hurt yourself, unless the suricanes had holes where you could put your fingers in, like bowling balls. But he didn't think that would work. He decided that suricanes were thrown with "special gloves," and he was very satisfied with this solution. He concluded:

P: It's a game about little monsters that were evolving and gaining more powers but could also lose them.
A: It's like when you grow up: you gain some things but lose others. On the one hand, you feel like a puppy/a little boy who wants to grow up; on the other hand, you feel like a red toad-horse/an angry boy because you don't want to grow and you don't want others to have milk and baby sleep. Evolving/growing is difficult.

P. listened carefully and told me:

P: You know, once I was on the beach and there were two men lying in the sun. One said to the other: "What a good life!", as if life were always like this!

He laughed a lot and so did I, surprised by the association he made.

The "eat, drink, and sleep" represented the growth that was felt by P. as poisonous. His sister was a little monster who appeared to him and received care he didn't experience. But the psychic nourishment he received there was less and less felt as dangerous. He found "special gloves" to handle the suricanes, allowing the balls with spikes/interpretations to circulate between the two of us, as if he had found a way to deal with growth without feeling threatened.

In another session, he put a pencil behind his ear to look like a man who designs houses. The pencil, a phallic symbol, was his desire to be a man in a constructive sense. Over the course of several sessions, he collected materials, took measurements, took notes, and at the end, invited me to see the house he had built.

In the session with the parents, they reported that P. continued to retain his feces at school and did not blow his nose, as if he was afraid of getting dirty. I told them that it was as if, by retaining the feces and secretions, P. wanted to hide the dirt, things from him that he thought we didn't tolerate. The mother said that days before, she was caressing P., and he got very excited and ended up biting her shirt on the chest, despite asking him to stop. Contrary to what was usual, she had managed to remain calm and explain to him that she knew he hadn't done it with bad intentions but that, if he had stopped, he wouldn't have ruined her blouse. She concluded by telling me that she understood that P. needed this tolerance.

At this stage, P. spent an entire session writing: "Why do my father and mother punish me?" Progressively, the primitive, implacable, and cruel superego was giving way to a structuring superego – the impositions of parents, teachers, and the analyst could have a reason for being. In a movement, now more introjective than projective, P. wants to understand these limits and prohibitions.

A few weeks later, the mother reported a problem at school that she lamented because everything was going so well. During the session, P. lay down on the floor and said it was a very bad day. He had the idea of throwing the slide on the floor together with other boys. As the little ones were on top, one of them had gotten really hurt and had gone to show him his injuries.

In the session with the parents, the mother expressed concern about the incident. At the same time, she was satisfied that she had reprimanded her son without losing control. She had also managed to deal with the teacher's stiffness, whereas a year ago, she would have felt distressed and helpless. The father reinforced that what happened did not invalidate all of his son's positive development.

I appreciated the fact that P., this time, spoke about what had happened and did so because he was worried and not because we made him do it. He had also assumed his responsibilities and had not used the fact that he had been helped by others to minimize what he had done. I also highlighted that by remaining calm, the mother had prevented her son from getting scared and wanting to free himself from his guilt.

In the next session, P. closed the blinds, turned off the lights, and asked me to turn on a spotlight and point it in his direction, which reminded me of an interrogation situation. Then he asked me to turn off the spotlight, and we were both left in the shadows. We started a fight. P. said he had been shot and had been half asleep. He moved from one side to the other, and even though he was hidden, he was restless, saying that his enemies were chasing him.

A: This game looks like a nightmare.
P: And it is!

A: Sometimes you want to stay in the dark, you don't want to see what bothers you. But ideas haunt you, like thinking about what could have happened to the little ones on the slide.

He listened very attentively. Then he got up and went to open the curtains. The next day he wanted to play the same fight and shots game, this time with the blinds open. After shooting me, P. examined me thoroughly and spent a long time treating me. I told him that when we have light/when we think about what we do, we can be scared, but we can also fix what we did.

In the following sessions, we continued fights with multiple weapons that I should list and count several times. At the end, he ordered me: "Memorize!" He asked me to repeat the weapons lists, and he repeated them too, many times, and said again: "Memorize it!" Meanwhile, he told the story of a warrior on whom a master cast a spell. When facing the fire, the warrior's horse died, but he managed to save himself.

P. was strengthening himself with the master/analyst, he was there looking for weapons/defenses that would protect him from the dangers he had to face. He was increasingly able to carry these weapons inside him by memorizing/internalizing what he experienced there.

In one session, he wondered about the Twin Towers: what year they were destroyed, how and why, whether people, children, and babies had died, and what was left there. I answered him simply and ended by saying that I thought they had made a plaque with the names of those who died. He became very thoughtful and decided to do math as if he were doing the math on his life, trying to understand himself. He could be destructive, but he could also be destroyed like those people in the towers. And what would happen afterward? Would he be reborn?

The next day, he draws the plaque that would replace the Twin Towers.

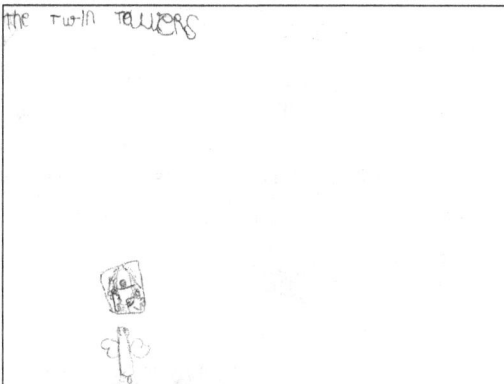

Figure 3.5

He explained that they were the remains of the towers, and a person watching. He asked me to make a copy to take to school, and during the rest of the session, he reproduced in the drawing the names of the people who died. He still needed a twin/ double, as he wasn't fully able to save it in memory. As in the drawing, in which there was an observer and an observed, he needed to observe these movements of destruction (the destruction of the towers/his destructiveness) and construction (the construction of the houses/internal structure that we were building there).

In a session before the Christmas break, he wanted to play a game of houses on paper. Shortly after, he said he had no home. He turned the game into a chase in which he was a giant snake that ran after me to eat me with devouring noises while urging me to run away.

He felt like he was going to be left without that house and that made him so hungry that he was afraid he would destroy me.

When he resumed his analysis, P. realized that the curtains were new. After almost being destroyed, and after the struggles to take the analyst with him, our tower remained intact and reinvested. Excitedly, he told me that his grandmother had given him a "real watch." Would P. accept the hours of reality, like adults, or would he keep the hours of his desire?

In the following sessions, he invented competitive games between the two of us. When I confronted him about trying to trick me, he agreed to play without cheating. He encouraged me to be aggressive and didn't believe me when I said I was tired. During a car race, he told me:

P: Pretend I won the race and you got furious.
A: As sometimes happens to you.

P. was in a dilemma between wanting me to be the winner, a strong figure of identification, or him being the winner, not giving up his infantile omnipotence. To give up childhood omnipotence, he should give up the idealization of his father. He was confronting reality and realizing that I did not correspond to the idealization he had made. It was a first attempt to resolve the oedipal conflict.

After a few days, he proposed that we play animals and chose to be "a wolf-like dog"; I chose to be a giraffe. He turned into a tiger and said he was going to attack me. I changed it to an elephant, and he bit my paw saying: "There is no animal more dangerous than the tiger!" I decided to transform myself into a penguin. P. was overjoyed by this idea and wanted to be a penguin too.

P: Now I would go to my house and you would go to yours . . . What are you doing?
A: I'm laying eggs.
P: Little eggs! Babies! Me too! How many do you have?
A: I have three. And you?
P: I have five!

The growing aggressivity led P. to be relieved when I introduced the penguin. He was thus able to move from the dangerous aggressive to the symbolic expression of strength, potency, through motherhood, the number of babies of each one.

In the session with the parents, they highlighted how P. was able to listen and to collaborate with household chores. His mother noticed in him the need to measure forces with his father. I valued his attitude in allowing, without getting angry, that his son competed with him and asserted himself in his masculinity without ceasing to show him who the grown man was.

At this point, P. began to play griffon vultures, "lions with eagle wings," "creatures that do not lay eggs" and fight using "paw and wing strokes."

The griffin, a symbol of psychic bisexuality, represented the transition from mother to father. Having confirmed that he had a penis, that he was not a woman, P. began to accept the generation gap.

That month, I had to cancel three sessions, which was well tolerated by P., who resumed the games as if there had been no break. He was better able to keep the analyst inside him. He was, progressively, tolerating separations better and defending himself in a more elaborate way.

In one game, he wanted to be a very small animal that would enter my body and cut my tubes so that I could only be with him. However, he himself concluded that, perhaps, we would both die. He then chose to be a little monster who was lost, and I should be a giant who passed by him and did not see him. When I found him, he tenderly leaned his forehead against mine and said: "Now I can go to rest."

P. had also been lost. Sometimes he wanted to be small like his little sister, other times he wanted to be big like his father. He discovered that he was no longer a baby but that he was still a child; he was not yet grown up, but he was a boy and one day he would be a man like his father. He could rest now.

P: Do you know that I'm now six years old? Do you know that I already know how to ride a bike alone without training wheels? It was my father who taught me. And I made a cake for my mother. She liked it very much.

After eighteen months of analysis, P.'s parents said that he did not look the same and that family life had changed globally. My proposal to reduce the frequency of sessions to two per week was felt as confirmation of the growth of the child and of themselves as parents.

In the following session, P. wanted to add 2,660 to 2,660. He wrote the numbers on a piece of paper and asked me to do the math, but he was not convinced by the result. Then he did the calculation himself. He ended up concluding that sum was well done. It was as if he was reflecting on this new sum of the two sessions per week. What result would it have?

The following month, the grandmother told me, with great affection, that her grandson had told her that, before, he came three times a week to be happier. Now, he was going to start coming only two because he was already much happier!

P. kept psychoanalysis on a two times per week frequency until he completed two years of analysis. He presented a progressive use of dialogue. The games became more of a sharing than a competition. There was a greater capacity for mentalization, better integration, a more organized thought and less invaded by the internal world, the phantasmatic more separated from the real.

The analyst offered herself as a malleable medium object (Roussillon, 2000). Through her continent function, she allowed the expression of P.'s hate, related to the object's failures (Winnicott, 1965), and presented herself as a support for the processes of symbolization.

The analytical work with the parents, centered on their relationship with the child, was an essential part of the treatment (Prat, 2014). The analyst respected the parents' requests so as not to reinforce the insecurity they felt in their parenting abilities but, at the same time, was attentive, anticipating their needs for contention of anxiety, especially following their son's aggressive impulsive acts at school.

P. was now more able to adapt to reality and to use his superego and defensive system in relation to sexuality and aggressivity. He was preparing to enter the latency phase.

Note

To conceptualize my work, I drew upon the following psychoanalytic authors: René Roussillon (2000), D. W. Winnicott (1965), and Régine Prat (2014).

Chapter 4

From scribble to sphinx

Originary phantasies as a symbolic matrix

Ana Belchior Melícias

The originary, the primitive, the archaic, the primary, are foundational themes for psychoanalysis and for humanity in general. How do we come into being? Where did we come from? What is our lineage? This mistery is wisely posed by Agostinho da Silva: "Life does not begin/No one knows where it came from/Perhaps breast gives the milk/Perhaps milk creates the breast" (Silva & Santos, 1995).

Laplanche and Pontalis (1986, 1988) argue that originary phantasies, or proto-phantasies, are responses to inquiries about origins: corresponding to the immediate origin of the subject is the phantasy of intrauterine life; to the origin of the subject's birth is the phantasy of the primal scene, to the origin of sexuality (considered trau-matic in itself) corresponds the phantasy of seduction, and the origin of the difference of sexes is organized in the phantasy of castration. In the phantasmatic trilogy of the oedipal drama, the phantasy of the primal scene is the prototype of the originary phantasies, incorporating the phantasies of seduction and castration with various combinations in the complex and dynamic network that organizes itself.

The phantasies of incorporation and expulsion are introduced by Freud as general organizers of psychic life. He also discusses the phantasy of the return to the womb and the phantasy of the family romance but does not assign them structural value. Some authors argue that one essential phantasy of the oedipal drama is missing from this trilogy, which holds a founding anthropological value: the parricidal phantasy.

According to Freud, the originary phantasies contain answers to all enigmas, constituting the paradigm of the quest for knowledge. They occupy a central place in the explanations that the child tries to construct regarding birth and sexuality, acquiring an organizing function in the psyche, serving curiosity and the need for knowledge. The phantasy of the primal scene is first named by Freud in his letter of May 2, 1897, to Fliess, and interestingly, shortly thereafter, that summer, he begins his self-analysis in search of his own origin. Sztulman (2004, p. 90) tells us: "To the fundamental enigma that questions, in the depths of their intimacy and des-tiny, men and societies, the originary phantasies offer a solution in a representative form, modeled on collective myths." He continues (Sztulman, 2004, p. 91): "Just as the dream does not find its navel, man can never know his beginning, his origin, which nevertheless will never abandon him."

DOI: 10.4324/9781003584018-5

Laplanche and Pontalis (1986) also consider that "the effort of Freud and the entirety of psychoanalytic reflection consists precisely in trying to explain the stability, the efficacy, the relatively organised nature of the individual's phantasmatic life." (p. 229). Therefore, originary phantasies or proto-phantasies are unconscious schemes and mnemic traces inherited – phylogenetic heritage – and for Freud, "the first matrix, classifying and organising the already present or forthcoming unconscious contents" (Sztulman, 2004, p. 89).

The complex psychic organization of the phantasmatic trilogy, composing the primal scene, condenses for Laplanche and Pontalis (1988) the traumatic intrusion of adult sexuality into the child's psyche: "What does the primal scene represent for us? The conjunction between the biological fact of conception (and birth) and the symbolic fact of filiation, between the 'wild act' of coitus and the existence of a triad: mother-child-father" (pp. 61–62).

But we all know that the most fundamental traumas are likely not of a sexual nature but rather of a narcissistic nature. According to Perron-Borelli (1997),

> the phantasy appears as a means of elaborating the trauma. Its function is to link and elaborate traumatic experiences that are therefore primarily quantitative, to "qualify" them, we might say, through representation . . . A trauma of separation or mourning may express itself (be elaborated) in a phantasy of seduction, of the primal scene, or of castration. (pp. 184–185)

He continues (1997):

> The originary phantasies, as psychic organisers, have the potential to link, in the order of the sexual, the most fundamental narcissistic traumas . . . To place in sexual representations and to invest libidinally what essentially threatens the needs of the self: needs for security, love, and narcissistic recognition from others. (p. 193)

For Klein (1928/1997, 1945/1996) and the post-Kleinians (Hinshelwood, 1992), the early Oedipus submits the primal scene to the sadistic drives of the paranoid-schizoid position. Through projective/intrusive identification, and its correlative seduction, sadistic phantasies (oral, urethral, and anal) translate into the concreteness of attacking the mother's body, to control, possess, and empty it, with the unsettling counterpart of the respective retaliatory phantasies of castration. Klein believes that "we can never grant sufficient importance, in the analysis of children, to the pressure of compulsion on the phantasy and its translation through action" (Klein, 1926, p. 161).

Thus, the Oedipus, as a secondary elaboration of fundamental narcissistic failures linked to immaturity and childhood impotence, refers back to the experience of abandonment, exclusion, frustration, separation, and mourning, that is, to the filling of a narcissistic lack or an object loss:

The phantasy of the primal scene depicts the representation that the child makes of a sexual intercourse between the parents; it is generally interpreted by the child as an aggressive, violent act, in a sadomasochistic relationship and as anal coitus within the framework of infantile sexual theories; it provokes in the child an extreme excitement that will later serve as a support for castration anxiety. (Sztulman, 2004, p. 90)

The phantasy of castration, as the axis of the oedipal conflict, will thus inherit all experiences of separation and pre-oedipal loss in the famous axis: breast–feces–penis–babies–money.

Green (2000) suggests that it is necessary to separate the originary from the phantasy. In the originary ("Ur"), there is no possibility of representation. The phantasies present themselves as symbolic matrices in the encounter of originary schemes with experience:

Insofar as the schemes do not provide contents, but only mediations that allow the contents, in the forms of phantasy and narration, to unfold. In this sense, as a structural mark, they allow individual experience to be inscribed. Green considers them temporal markers that organize and historicize events. (Sverdlik, 2010, p. 39)

They would thus be ready, interconnected, originary schemes, through which new experiences can gain meaning. The most organizing are those that allow for a large number of representations, granting them a certain coherence.

I would conclude that the originary phantasies, presenting themselves as a symbolic matrix, allow for the figurability/narrativity of emotional experience at three levels: historical, objectal, and of the functioning of the analytical couple in the psychoanalytical process.

Enzo

With the entry into first grade, Enzo, a six-year-old boy, experiences great suffering, as he cannot separate from his parents or stay with strangers. The parents report that

despite being extraordinarily gentle and affectionate, he has always struggled to integrate into new environments. He either does not integrate at all or becomes so excited that he is socially unpleasant. In sports, he will give up right after the first lesson. He shows no interest in anything.

E. has a younger brother. One of the parents is a native English speaker. They arrive through a psychoanalyst colleague, who has E.'s father in psychotherapy due to depression. In touch with his feelings, the father says: "Until now, I've never allowed myself the luxury of feeling, and I am searching for my identity. I don't

like my job even though I am very successful, and the marriage is not secure."
Work and love, the two axes of mental health, seem to place him in front of the
sphinx, in search of his origin and history. He states that "he spends his life putting
out fires" and that "a place, like this consulting room, is what I need . . . to stay still
and calm."

The mother says, "I was with a psychologist because I was also depressed, but
I don't think that's for me. I like to be practical and solve things quickly." She feels
that the marital relationship began to cool with the birth of the second child, and
despite being depressed, she uses manic defenses to soothe her pain.

Both present histories that reveal serious early failures due to traumatic separations and abandonments that have not been sufficiently elaborated.

I find myself imagining E.' s difficulty in finding his place within this family
and in internally organizing the traumatic and encrypted experiences of his parents:
transgenerationality inhabits him like a foreign and senseless body.

As Freud (1917/1976) pointed out the "psychic reality is the decisive reality"
(p. 430), I question myself in a working-through process: how will he internally
live the experience of separation? What place does he feel he occupies within his
parents? What internal space can he construct for his parents? How can he evolve
from the narcissistic dyad to oedipal triangulation? How can latency and schooling
be organized in light of contamination by such early issues?

Throughout the entire analytical process with E., the parents remain distant,
with no openness for transformation and without requesting sessions to think
about the issues that were troubling them. They end up separating, and despite
feeling E.'s improvements after one and a half years, they interrupt his analysis. As Meltzer (1967) points out, one of the three types of ending to analytic
work is "the interruption for external reasons that is in fact the usual outcome
of child analysis, except where the parents have been analysed themselves"
(p. 51).

Initial sessions

First session

The mother fears that E. will not be able to be alone with me, and when they arrive,
he starts crying and stomping. I introduce myself and show him where the room is,
and we go in. E. cries with sobs but begins to respond to my questions, albeit with
some resistance.

He repeatedly says,

E: I want my mum . . . I don't want to be here.
A: Do you know why you came here?
E: I don't know.
A: Your parents are worried.
E: That's a lie!

A: I can see your great suffering, and it seems to me that's why your parents brought you.

E: That's a lie!

A: So I'm here today to hear your truth.

He slips off the couch onto the floor, lying on his stomach with his head buried in his arms, between the sofa and the bookcase. I sense a uterine atmosphere and a potential birthing experience. I remain silent. His crying begins to calm down.

Here and there, I talk and tell him that I imagine how distressful this situation is for him.

E: I don't stay with strangers.

A: It seems fair that you feel this way, since I'm still a stranger to you.

E: Yes!

A: Who do you feel good with?

E: With my mum, my brother, my dad, and my maid.

A: And at school?

E: Also.

I then take an interest in school and ask if he plays any sports. As he does not respond, I playfully start guessing:

A: Swimming?

E: No.

A: Tennis?

E: No.

A: Soccer?

E: No.

A: Basketball?

E: No.

A guessing game begins that he enjoys, and while still on the floor, he turns over onto his back. I can now see his face. He challenges me to keep playing the guessing game about sports, saying,

E: It starts with R.

A: Rugby?

He laughs affirmatively.

A: Do you have friends at school?

E: It starts with F.

A: Filipe.

He waits, looking at me, urging me to continue.

A: What do you like to play?
E: It starts with N.
A: Oh, that one is harder.
E: Nintendo, Mario's game.
A: Guessing is like playing games . . . I can try to guess some things and get lucky, but I can't guess the things you think . . . and we'll see if when you know me better, you can tell me. For now, you like it when I guess . . . Like babies do . . .
E: I'm Enzo poop!

He laughs with loud and disproportionate laughter.

A: Maybe you came here to show me this baby-poop and for us to take care of him, but I also know you have a more grown-up side that can tell me things, play, draw, so I can get to know Enzo C. P. (saying his first name and surnames)
E: I'm going to write my name.

He gets up, goes to the table, and tries to write his full name but is not satisfied, crumpling the paper and throwing it on the floor.

After some pre-birth time in our relationship, E. accepts talking about what bothers him. I am a stranger to him, and we are getting to know each other exploratorily through a guessing game. Through *rêverie* and a primary maternal-analytical concern, we become interested in each other: who is this baby, and who is this analyst (mother–father) who is there with him?

He initially presents himself as Enzo-poop, anally coloring this first and primordial encounter with the object. I accept Enzo-poop, but likely feeling countertransference from his unbearable pain of separation acted out there, I potentially present to him a more grown-up boy, with his first name alongside his last names (maternal and paternal), inscribing him in his identity and history, opening the way for the phantasmatization of his origin.

E. tries to write his full name, still facing difficulties and gaps. Not reflecting reality, he ends his last name with "n o t." Could it be the "no" of our relationship that is still strange to him? The "no" of his difficulty and simultaneously an attempt to separate from the object? The "no" of his Enzo-baby-poop phantasy? The "no" of Spitz, as the third organizer of the object relationship development (Houzel, Emmanuelli and Moggio, 2004)?

E: Is it time to go home yet?
A: I still have time for you.

E. decides to draw.

E: Here I am, and here is my Mum. Huge. Look at her eyes. Here is the pee-pee. She's making pee.

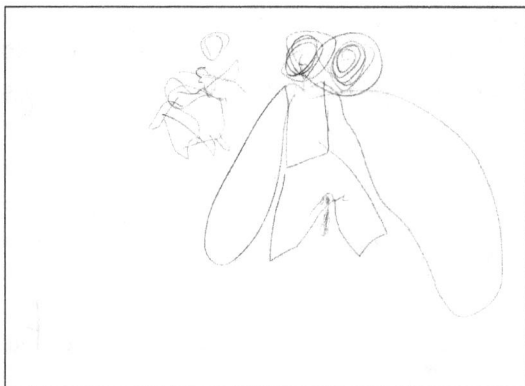

Figure 4.1

We are starting to be two through the dialogue made possible by the drawing. Him and me. Him and the mother. He is absolutely confused and entangled in a persecutory gaze (mine? the mother's as sensed at birth?) and in an anal-urethral state, which already signals, in our relationship, the precariousness of his internal organization, the pregenital confusion translated in the rawness of this drawing, and the force of the archaic sadistic phantasies that disorganize him. But he also reveals some trust in the possibility of containment in our relationship. As Aberastury (1982) considers, from the very beginning of an analysis, the child introduces both the phantasy about their own suffering and the phantasy about what they need to be healed.

He has a speech articulation problem, which seems to me to be more of a babyish speech than a true impairment. There is also latent excitement and impulsivity, ready to erupt.

E. continues and makes a new drawing, saying as he does:

E: It's my family. Look, Dad has growing ears.

Figure 4.2

In working through, I find myself dreaming: do they grow because Dad decided to listen to himself better, considering the possibility of being helped? Because he felt heard by the father who brought him to me? My ears grow in my effort to listen to him/myself?

E: My brother has huge hair and a crest. He doesn't need a hat.

The "rooster man" (Ferenczi, 1913/1992), entangled in narcissistic-oedipal confusions, doesn't need extra protections, other defenses.

E: I am so tiny (third figure from left to right) with a huge head and lots of hair around.

He intrauterinely, so baby-poop, so small and dependent, compensated with a big head, protected by hair – superhuman strength like Samson – denying possible castration? Protection against true thoughts?

E: Here is Mum. She is in love with Dad.

E., excluded from this passion, translates it through a lightning bolt, a parental relationship he imagines and experiences as electric and stormy, as is the tension at the beginning of our relationship.

While I take note of his description behind the drawing, E. seems thoughtful and surprised by my interest in him.

He successively asks me in a torrent,

E: Ana, can a person know everything? Mum says she knows everything. Ana, is there magic? Ana, can a person know what another person is thinking? My maid says she knows what I'm thinking. Why did my parents send me here?

A: It seems that now you are showing me your six-year-old side with curiosities, not understanding things that parents decide . . ., not yet realizing what you are doing here with me. Good questions, E., for us both to think about and discover together.

The time has ended, and E. sees the toy box that has always been there. He wants to look inside. I say he will come back two more times.

Second session

I hear screams on the street: "I'm not going, I'm not going. I don't want to!"

E. arrives out of control.

E: I'm not going, I don't want to, muuuummm!

The mother firmly tells him that she is leaving, takes him to the room, and shuts the door. He screams, throws himself to the floor, rolls around on the rug, flailing his legs and arms like a newborn, in uncontainable despair. One of his sneakers flies off.

He sits in the opposite corner of the room, on the floor with his back to me, facing the shelf, and screams:

E: I hate Mum!!!
A: And perhaps me too.

He cries with shouts and sobs, dragging his nails across the sisal rug on the floor. This crying lasts practically the entire session, gradually decreasing over time.

He keeps his back to me, turned toward the shelf. From time to time, I say something to him, unsure if my words can contain him: It's hard for babies to be separated from their mothers; they feel torn away; babies become desperate when their mothers leave, they aren't sure if their mothers think about them when they're gone, or when they're with Dad; sometimes you show your suffering, sometimes it seems I feel your fury because Mum doesn't obey you; if only you could command her, she would always be where you wanted; I am here waiting for you, on the outside, trying to understand what's going on inside you, what you feel, what you're thinking; I can wait as long as you need until that desperate baby wants to play, draw, talk, think.

Very gradually, the crying diminishes in intensity. E. starts pulling cotton balls from his socked foot. He begins to flick those mini-balls, throwing them against the shelf, as if playing marbles. I say with satisfaction and a sense of relief,

A: Ah, now it seems this baby E. is doing what all babies do when they are away from their mothers . . . playing.

He turns his face toward me and smiles brightly without saying anything. I felt a great relief, and now that communication is open, I say to him:

A: We don't have more time today to play with the toys here.

E. runs to me and says,

E: Where are they?

He looks at the toy box that had been on the floor since the beginning and eagerly starts picking up the toys, beginning to talk to me:

E: Will I come back?
A: Now we need to decide together. If you want, I have a time for you on Thursday.
E: I want to come.
A: And I will be here waiting for you. You can come as a baby like today, or more grown-up, wanting to play. I'll wait for you, and we'll see what we can play with and think about together.

He takes his time putting on the sneaker that had flown off at the beginning. He leaves feeling very light and relieved.

E. comes very regressed, enacting the terrible anxieties of separation and object loss, showing me his feelings of helplessness and despair, and simultaneously his fury for not being able to control the object. Archaic phantasies, archaic anxieties, archaic object relationships. We are in the realm of the primary phantasies with their usual concreteness and violence, without the mediation of fantasy-imagination-dream. Transgenerationality – traumatic early separations in both parents' childhoods – seems to be enacted by him, like beta elements without the containment of an alpha function.

Third session

He arrives five minutes late, along with his mother. He smiles when he sees me. The mother is surprised to see E. enter, so different from the two previous sessions.

He goes straight to the toy box and dumps all the toys on the floor, leaving only the family figures inside, which is significant. He curiously opens the barrels (seven barrels that fit together like Russian Matryoshkas dolls) and closes them with focus and skill. On the floor, he sets up a play scenario with the barrels, cars, toy figures, and animals. In the playing, there are fences with animals, and the toy figures form groups that steal from and violently attack each other. There's a certain confusion, such as putting cows with lions, not separating domestic or farm animals from wild ones, and an indiscriminate relationship between the figures, whose roles he cannot define or maintain. The roles (Klein, 1929/1996) quickly reverse: what attacks becomes attacked, what steals becomes stolen, etc. There's a constant restlessness and excitement, and the narrative he tries to enact becomes muddled and falls apart in successive failed attempts. He loses the thread of the story, restarting and introducing

new situations that unravel without being able to proceed or satisfactorily conclude different plays, revealing a failure of symbolization and a confusion of
aggressive and sadistic phantasies that block his thinking, dismantling the play.
However, he is entertained and creatively finds some solutions, persistently
trying to organize his inner confusion, showing his good potential and a desire
to understand.

Due to school scheduling conflicts, we start the analytical process twice a
week.

At this beginning, I observe this new infant/child. I try to find a place for him by
clarifying how I should engage with him, what his needs are, and the right words
for effective communication.

I found in his folder three drawings from this period of the early sessions
that E. did not want to discuss. In hindsight, they seem quite enlightening
and synthesizing of what we were experiencing, even without being named,
thought about, or shared, but only acted out in his attempts to organize playing that fell apart: playing as discharge, with great excitement, featuring cruel
and terrifying characters, confusion of structuring splits (inside and outside,
good and bad, self and other, big and small, boys and girls), and great omnipotence in the magical scenes he staged. These drawings are done in pencil with
faint and insecure strokes, revealing on one hand the fragility of his psychic
organization but also his insecurity and distrust in the containing capacity of
my mind.

Figure 4.3

Scribbles (Figure 4.3) are a primitive and still undifferentiated expression of
drawing, where the representation is more about sensory scrawling as a pulsional
discharge (Klein, 1930/1996) than about the possibility of expressing thoughts,
phantasies, and desires.

Figure 4.4

A partial and incomplete object, (Figure 4.4) without a face and empty, but where the body-heart reveals his need for affection and the exchanges he might desire in our relationship, which still feels insecure to him.

Figure 4.5

And finally, this boy with a superhero cape, without feet and hands, (Figure 4.5) seems to me, *a posteriori*, a faithful portrait of E. that I am getting to know better: fragile, with his cape that grandiosely and maniacally protects him, castrated of feet and hands, highlighting his lack of autonomy and stability, as well as his difficulties in making connections with others.

Last two weeks before summer vacation

He missed the last session without notifying, and when they arrived, his mother explained she had spent the weekend alone with her husband and hadn't arranged for him to be brought over.

E. enters feeling distressed and disconnected. This separation caught both of us off guard, leaving us without knowing about each other. He begins taking out boxes to play but loses focus and decides to draw.

In a sketch of evolutionary and progressive movement, E. seeks to contain and represent our separation from his parental couple through drawing, channeling the pre-oedipal tone that these discontinuities evoke. He begins accessing imaginary scenarios he hadn't managed to reach through the previously attempted disorganizing and frustrating games.

Figure 4.6

E: Ana peeing and here's the butt pooping. I'm dizzy today. (laughs) I drank wine. No, no, I didn't drink anything.
A: It seems like you feel drunk on crazy ideas.
E: That's it. Drunk. Crazy.

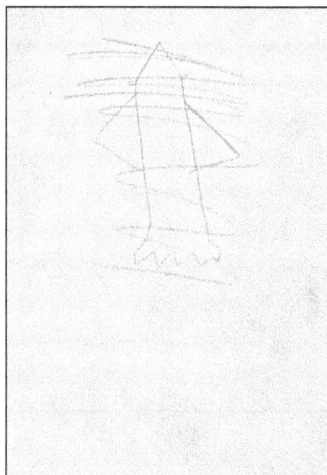

Figure 4.7

E: It's a rocket. The wing got crooked.

A: Here, too, it seems something turned out crooked, broken, from you not coming to our last session. Perhaps you feel like everything here got crooked too?

E: You became. Crooked.

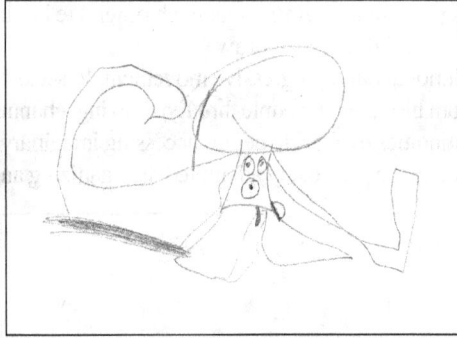

Figure 4.8

E: Ana out on the street completely naked, showing her boobies, butt, and pee-pee.

A: Who was I with in the last session? Maybe you're already worried about the vacation we'll have here . . . wondering with whom shall I be during vacations?

E: When is it?

I review the dates with him, while he draws.

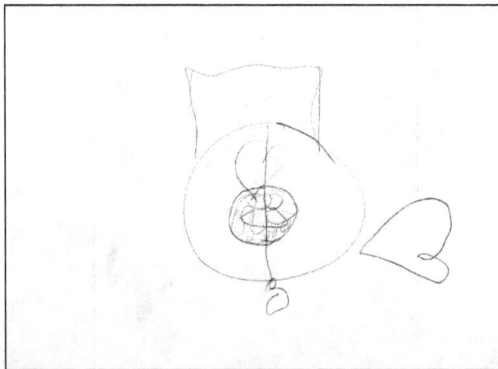

Figure 4.9

E: My butt with poop stuck in it. You love your poop, and you gave my butt a
little kiss – no, you gave your poop a kiss.

I continue in working through following Geissmann (1995): Am I capable of loving E. as the "poop-baby"? Am I able to contain this avalanche of such raw material? How can I metabolize these poop-thoughts, as a way to stay connected, even
if it's like stucked poop, so as not to feel the pain of separation: of him missing the
session; of his separation from his parents, and of the imminent separation as we
approach summer vacation? Neither fully inside nor outside? Is it an attack on the
relationship, which could be suddenly lost, like an anal castration? Primitive beta
elements emerge, filling the relationship with anality, with its movements of retention and expulsion, dominance and submission, and with geographic and zonal
confusion (Meltzer) arising from partial, voyeuristic, exhibitionistic, and sadistic
drives.

The vivid eroticization of sadistic, oral, anal, and phallic phantasies attacks the
mother's body, with phantasies of retaliation and destruction directed at that same
body, which prevents him from thinking. Within the claustrum of the maternal
body, the identification doesn't seem projective in the Bionian sense of communication but rather intrusive, as Meltzer has shown us.

Summer vacation. I've moved to a new consulting room, as had already been
scheduled and announced. Immediately after resuming, suddenly, due to unfore-
seen health reasons, I had to be absent for an additional two weeks.

When we finally met again, we began an intense and exhausting journey. E.,
deeply hurt by so many separations, expresses his anger provocatively, attacking my "body" through the room and the materials, testing my resilience and my
capacity for *rêverie*. I often feel overwhelmed countertransferentially by his enormous confusion, his inability to think, and our struggle to find a shared language.
He tests both my ability to contain his violent and sadistic attacks as well as my
paternal function of setting limits and protecting the "mother-room-body" from his
destructive, intrusive, and retaliatory movements typical of the paranoid-schizoid
position. He destroys various graphic materials to ensure I would provide more,
plundering the maternal body of its resources. He repeatedly throws a cushion
forcefully against the wall until it rips, spilling its contents on the floor. He insists
on taking some toys home, and on bringing others from his house to keep in his
box, becoming furious when I discriminate the spaces and boundaries for him,
refusing the constant merging of confused spaces. He threatens that if I don't let
him, he won't come back. He even leaves one day, holding me blackmailed at the
door: he'll either take a toy home at the end of the session, or he'll leave. He shows
me his body, wants to touch mine. He sings: "I'm sexy, and you know it." I sense
the promiscuity in his seduction, from his unwillingness to accept my differentiated
role, separate from him and his parents. I feel invaded by these boundary-crossing
attacks.

I recall Klein's teaching that the object is born in hate; it is partial and split
into a bad external object, with projective identification as the consequence of this

process and the mother's capacity for *rêverie*. I often feel that my own *rêverie* is blocked, preventing me from thinking, given the profusion of archaic phantasies, the chaotic disorganization of emotions, and uncontrollable actings out.

All evocation of the primal scene (Chouvier, 2004) nearly inevitably recalls experiences of abandonment, exclusion, frustration, separation, and mourning, referencing the filling of a narcissistic lack or an object loss. The castration phantasy thus becomes the heir to all experiences of separation and pre-oedipal loss – the trauma of birth, the weaning, the loss of feces, and the loss of the phallus. This chain of symbolic equivalents – breast, feces, penis, babies, money – indicates ongoing transformations, from the original loss of the breast to the castration phantasy central to the oedipal conflict.

In one session, E. tries to take home a chain of a toy by hiding it in his butt. The small ball attached by a chain condenses, like a dream, a breast-cord that either connects or destroys us. When I realize it, I ask him to remove it, and we agree that I will keep with me for a while some toys that have become source of constant disruptions. To my surprise, E. hands over these toys with relief, feeling that my paternal function is protective of our relationship, preventing him from possessing and controlling my "body-room-toys," and providing a boundary to his destructive functioning.

This moment marked a turning point, after which the castration anxiety experienced at a pregenital level seemed to diminish, along with the relief of his guilt for the phantasized damage inflicted on the object.

In the beginning, there was only action, dispersion, fragmentation, and confusion in his unsatisfactory play attempts, resulting from symbolic failure and the destructive level of his phantasies. Very gradually, E. begins to try, through drawing, to represent these phantasies that are so difficult to translate. He starts moving from the maternal, fusion-based world to the more differentiated paternal one – a more symbolized world, where acted-out play gives way to figurative representation, and a coherent narrative begins to take form.

Figure 4.10

He makes tiny books, cutting out pages and taping them together. The use of materials at his disposal for constructive purposes implies progress, which also emerges in his stories, where characters begin to take on figuration and narrative structure. The books start out very small (in the image, they're placed on an A4 sheet of paper), as if their small size magically protects him/us from the violence and the effects of the cruelty and destructiveness of the sadistic characters that frighten us both. It's interesting to observe the evolution over time. Gradually, the drawings will come to fill the entire page.

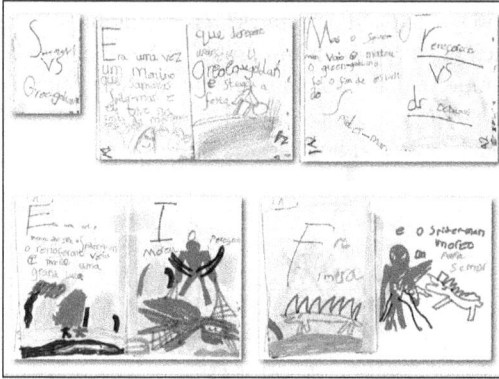

Figure 4.11

He creates a small book (in the image, on an A4 sheet) with two stories.

E: Spider-Man versus Green Goblin. Once upon a time, there was a boy named Spider-Man, and he was at Merigan's (Mary Jane's) party; suddenly, the Green Goblin appeared and ruined the party. But Superman came and killed the Green Goblin. That was the end of Spider-Man's story.

Without saying anything to him, since we are just beginning to experiencing a new relational mode, I try to follow his thinking effort, reflecting about his first story: a boy was at a friend's (girlfriend's) party, but his enemy comes and ruins it. The good-bad split is beginning to take form: one character is festive and connected to life, and another is a spoiler and destroyer, bringing a primal scene into focus where someone has to die. Could we think of parricide as a component phantasy of the oedipal conflict? Does my husband appear here, who in E.'s phantasy distances me from him during vacations and separations, spoiling our "party"?

The second story:

E: Rhino versus Dr. Octopus: Once upon a time, there was the boy Spider-Man. Rhino came, and they had a big fight. Rhino died.

He writes: *End* in one color and *Era* and *River* in another.

E: And Spider-Man died forever.

Is there already a boy anticipating a possible humanization? The scene of destruction-death and the anguish and guilt of this boy Spider-Man, over Rhino's death, leads to a confusion: the end of a story, the end of an era, is also the beginning of a new story. He needs to add another page for Spider-Man's "forever death" . . . "Died forever," so psychologically different from "They lived happily ever after," which feeds hope in endings with a future. Am I the octopus, without enough hands to manage these still so incipient narratives? His castration phantasies remain quite active, and his attempt to represent the primal scene is overtaken by drive force (death/castration anxiety) that disorganizes him: the boy Spider-Man has to die as punishment for his incestuous desires of fusion with the mother. Both the good and the bad die, in a place devoid of hope.

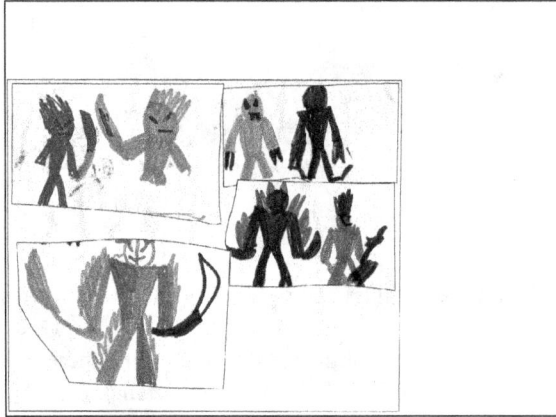

Figure 4.12

The characters then start being drawn on small pieces and later glued onto another piece of paper (still smaller than a full A4 sheet, as shown in the image), as if the full space of the page intimidates him. The sheet now serves as a boundary, a container for his contents, these still undifferentiated monster-heroes. With a lot of agitation and excitement, he talks about these characters, though I can't quite understand, and nor can he. My role, as a "toilet-mother," is to receive and contain, much like the sheet of paper itself, these frightening contents of his primary phantasies that were previously acted out, and to share the emotional experience between us – a process that sometimes frightens me too. I don't say much. I express interest, asking a few questions, as I notice he appreciates my effort to understand his drawings, and I take this opportunity to practice my negative capability. In time, we will come to better understand these terrifying characters, who, for now, are simply discharged and contained there.

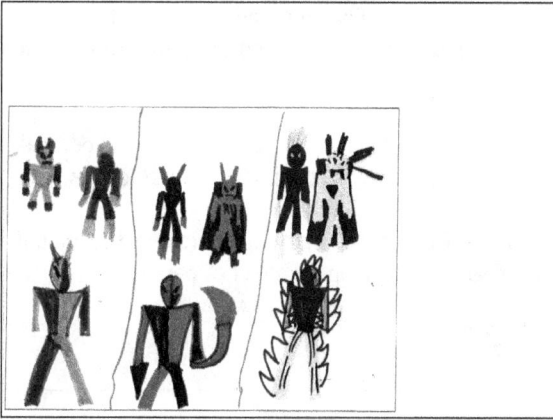

Figure 4.13

On a sheet smaller than a standard A4, but nearly normal size (See Figure 4.13), the same types of characters appear, but now more defined: divided into three groups, each group has three figures, and the character at the bottom blends the colors of the two above it. Vertical lines begin to organize spaces and triangulated families, and the phantasies of lineage (if they can be called so) start to reveal themselves. He is embedded in a story stemming from his maternal and paternal lineage. I notice the little heart on the clothing of one of the characters. Is this my desire? That we manage to connect these cruel, armed beings with more libidinal energy? Might these two vertically divided sides of the maternal and paternal clothing of the characters achieve complementarity in a desirable, healthy and vitalized primal scene?

He continues to draw on a sheet still smaller than A4, but there's now a story about a father and a son, which he narrates and allows me to write down:

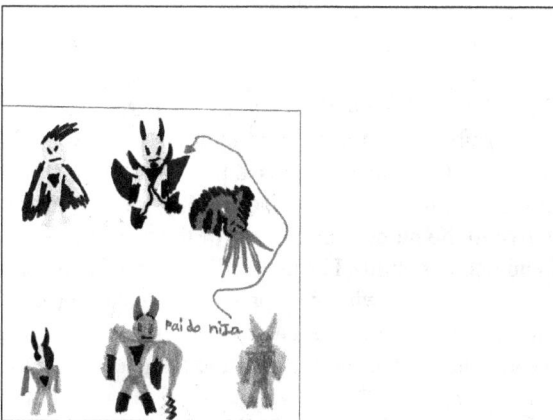

Figure 4.14

E: The father of the Ninja . . . The small colorful one (figure on the bottom left) had all the colors and powers and killed the father of the Ninja, who was the ruler of the world.

E. is gradually approaching the parricidal phantasy of his oedipal conflict, where the small figure, omnipotently invested with all colors/powers, kills the ruler of the world.

Somewhat detoxified from these terrifying characters that inhabit him, he finally ventures to make a drawing on an entire sheet of paper.

Figure 4.15

E: This is the Ninjas' airplane, with the giant, a friend of the Ninja's father. The sea is full of crocodiles and sharks.

He illustrates the "gigantic" retaliation against his parricidal wish: the threat of castration to the airplane-penis, represented by the crocodiles and sharks that fill this sea and E.'s imagination. But now, at last, the Ninja's father has friends – parts of him that begin to care for and take responsibility for the harm inflicted on the other. I am sensitive to the number on the tail of the airplane: 2 1 1. The two parents, one child, and another child? The possibility that he is now increasingly able to organize his internal objects with an expanded secondary process? Still, he and the mother are united in fusion (2), excluding the father and brother (1, 1)? The two of us, closer together in our work (2), while also becoming more individualized and clarified (1, 1)?

The upcoming separation (Christmas holidays) will be experienced in a much more processed way than the one in summer.

Figure 4.16

In the last session before the holidays, Enzo makes a drawing like a greeting card, which reassures me about his possibility to humanize and to value, like all children, the cultural myth of Christmas, as a myth of origin, of family, and triangulation.

Figure 4.17

Just to be safe, E. also creates a "Christmas police to arrest those who steal the presents," making it clear that his active part of his desire to steal presents from the maternal body (breast–penis–babies–money) is now protected by a Christmas policeman. Thus, the two of us head into the holidays feeling more secure. There's now a father-police figure who stands in the way of this uncontrollable drive. Is he starting to internalize a good police-father who protects him from his desires and his bad internal objects?

We resume our work, now meeting three times a week. E. arrives eagerly and dives into his drawings, entering a period of long and deep elaboration.

Figure 4.18

E: The Riddler, plus the Joker, plus the Clown-Lady were stealing jewels from a store. The police came and arrested them all. The police helicopter took the bags of stolen goods. I have the Joker toy. I'll bring it so you can see.

In this first session after the Christmas holidays, he revisits the theme of thieves and the police, thus reestablishing our connection. However, the characters chosen, now an oedipal trio, seem to reflect what is happening at the level of his internal conflict and, naturally, within our relationship as well: there's now a Riddler-Enzo, representing the epistemophilic instinct – curious and persistent, attempting to organize his primal phantasies within an expanding framework of symbolic and creative capacity. We have the Joker-father (the villain from Batman), an ambivalent figure with a cynical smile, but also a card that plays in many games, embodying numerous possibilities. Finally, we have the Clown-Lady-mother, a more undifferentiated and foolish side, dressed like a joker, symbolizing perhaps his growing awareness of the connection and quality of his parents' love.

Figure 4.19

In the next session, he continues clarifying these roles and inner qualities within the oedipal triad. (See figure 4.19)

E: The car is coming out of the box and returning to the track. On the track, there's another Ferrari. If one wins and the other loses, they both win because they're on the same team. These two cars crashed and are being repaired.

At last, we have a primal scene represented in human terms. The team, as a sign of the increasing collaboration possibility between us, between him and his parents, him and his brother, and between his internal objects, leads him from a world of retaliatory competition to one of healthy competition. The repair and restoration of his damaged internal objects suggest a transformation from a sadistic primal scene to a more flexible one, with the potential for healing.

Figure 4.20

After visiting the landscape of cooperation-repair, we regressively return to the sadistic primal scene, with all its raw elements that, however, the analytical field and his mind are now able to contain, represent, and narrate:

E: The spaceship went to space, and when it was landing, it malfunctioned. A piece came off, this red triangle, and there were four crew members. One jumped out with a parachute and a bag full of another man's blood who was jabbed.
A: He was jabbed?
E: On Earth and in space, there are always invisible spikes. Look here. (he draws the spikes) Another one was dressed like a bird, a rocket man, and he had

metal gloves because the landing strip had spikes and a lot of blood because many people had already died there. Another one fell and broke his neck and is covered in blood everywhere. The pilot is strapped in by the belt to the spaceship, only his legs are outside, and his shoes fell off.

A: What do you think will happen to him?

E: He's going to die because the spaceship is going to crash. He can't land. And the tip of this wing fell off.

The four crew members of his family-spacecraft continue to be unable to reach the ground, and in their attempt to humanize themselves, they end up dying. The spikes, the broken neck, the blood, the trapped legs, the falling wing allude to castration and the impossibility for E. to land and step onto the solid ground of good objects and more reassuring and loving relationships.

However, the dynamism of these progressive and regressive movements, from Ps ↔ D and *vice versa*, allows for the nourishment of hope in the development of the alpha function of the mind and the struggle for creative and enriching movements to prevail over destructive and threatening ones. Projective identification now has a tone of communication and not solely discharge. The qualitative texture of the sessions is gaining the dimension of the pleasure of a real encounter between two differentiated individuals (no longer fused) who remain within each other's minds and to whom we can access through memory and imagination (rather than through intrusive identification). Gradually, we begin to experience the setting as a true intermediate and potential space, where both minds can create something that belongs to neither one nor the other, as Winnicott, Green, Ogden, and Ferro tell us in their deepening analytic filed and of the thirdness notion.

Figure 4.21

E: Look, I brought the Joker.

He shows me a Lego figure whose head spins and has two faces.

E: Can it stay here in my box?
A: You already know.
E: How do I do it?
A: That's great. Maybe we can think together now. Do you think you can draw it, and then the drawing stays, and you take the toy home?
E: Great! Then I will draw. (See Figure 4.21)

He carefully draws the two faces of the toy whose head spins, showing one face or the other. It's the first time E. asks for help and wonders how we could face his desire together. He receives my thoughts without anger or fury, accepting the limits of the setting/relationship without trying to pervert them, without attempting to seduce or retaliate against me. And there we stay with the Joker, with the ambivalence of good and evil in the same object in the process of totalization.

Figure 4.22

E. continues to delve deeper into the explorations of origin. He draws and tells a long and condensed story, the content of which, previously hinted at in the first story of the mini-book, can now be expanded and symbolized with greater elaborative richness.

E: This is Hagrid from Harry Potter. No, actually this one doesn't count. (he makes an X) They are Lego figures. I wanted to watch the Harry Potter movie with my dad, but he never has time. The Hat Man was the one who put him there. He pressed the wrong button and started to get bad.
A: It sounds complicated.

E: The Hat Man didn't want this; he just wanted him to have muscles. Here in the x-ray is his flying skateboard. Here in green, the mask. Behind the machine, there's a ladder that leads to a secret place, and up there, there's a wall with bombs and Harry's mask, the son of the Green Goblin, not Harry Potter's. He has a picture of the mask, his skateboard, his costume, the sword. The son Harry, in his imagination, broke the wall and threw a knife at his father. He was discovering that his father was evil and discovered the laboratory. The Green Goblin wanted to ruin the party of his best girlfriend.

A: It looks like you here with me, sometimes.

E. smiles. He continues to draw details and tells me,

E: Next to the secret place, there was their house. The Green Goblin lived there without the costume and Harry. Harry was wearing a red tie. The clothes are purple, and he has the basketball that his friend gave him.

A: Oh, he had a friend.

E: The friend was Peter Parker, who was Spider-Man. Harry is in the kitchen cooking for him and his dad to eat.

A: Where is the dad?

E: Now the dad was in the laboratory without him knowing.

A: Does he have to take care of his dad?

E: He has to take care of his dad, but only sometimes. Sometimes he has to take care of himself. Sometimes the dad makes breakfast. Here, Spider-Man was shooting webs because he saw the Green Goblin turning bad, and he wants to catch him so he doesn't hurt people. He picked up four bombs and is going to throw them, and the dad, the Green Goblin, can't get through, but with the flying skateboard, he can.

He continues the drawing and says,

E: Here's a tap and a bucket, and the water flows here in the pipe.

This key drawing of his elaboration condenses aspects of the growing discrimination of his mind: the bad ones are inside one space, and the good ones are outside – a creation of a "psychic envelope" where internal conflicts can be located and contained. Hagrid, the friendly giant and protector of children in the Harry Potter saga, already exists but is not yet integrated into the story, perhaps like the analyst. For the first time, he speaks of the father in relation to him: the father who does not have time to watch the Harry Potter saga with him, who does not ally himself with this adventure just like the boy Harry, who is also searching for his origin. Harry in his scenario is still the son of Spider-Man's archenemy, who, in turn, is his friend. And the sentence – "The son Harry . . . broke the wall and threw a knife at his father. He was discovering that his father was evil and discovered the laboratory" – besides the more immediate parricidal wishes, speaks of his need to investigate the inside of the father. From the intrusive thefts of treasure in the maternal territory,

Enzo now seems wishing to project himself into the discovery of the paternal: the masculine secrets, the muscles, the secret places, the laboratories, and the perception of lack. The father does not take care of him as he would like.

But what seems most important to me, and I consider it a leap, like the one Freud spoke of in "Two Principles" (1911), is the creation of the space of imagination and daydreaming – "in his imagination" – of the transition from the pleasure principle to the reality principle, the secondarization of the primary process we have been following until now, the progressive transformation of beta elements into alpha, and therefore a more developed *apparatus* for thinking thoughts with the corresponding containing function of the mind. Finally, I would just like to point out the end of the story, where E. installs a tap, as evidence of the progressive control of his previously uncontrollable impulsivity: a pipe emerges, where the water of imagination can circulate between the internal and external worlds, between phantasy and reality, between the more psychotic aspects of his mind and his healthier and more creative parts. Perhaps he is beginning to approach the benevolence of the giant Hagrid, so different from the giant Ninja.

Figure 4.23

In this session, E. enters and urgently grabs the papers. He divides a sheet into squares and starts drawing heroes. It's a drawing that has been revisited and expanded many times in the following sessions.

E: I'm just going to draw the ones I already have. I'll draw the hero, the name, the symbol, and the weapon.

In his search for affiliation and origin, E. begins to clarify primitive clusters and differentiate their qualities. By giving them a name, an identity-clothing, the symbol of their qualities and skills, and the weapon/resource that allows for attack or defense, he is organizing his thoughts. He flips the paper over and writes on the back: *All my Lego*. He continues the drawing of the heroes and later adds to it.

E: I'm also going to draw some that I don't have but would like to have.
E: Yes, we also have inside us what we wish we could have that hasn't happened, the things that are missing.
E: My parents are going to bring me these figures from Egypt, which aren't available in Portugal yet.

It seems that he can now tolerate immediate gratification, waiting for what he doesn't have, but also better enduring the lack, meaning he can handle the narcissistic absence that previously filled him in a manic and omnipotent way. Besides the name, the symbol, and the weapon that he asks me to write/organize on a sheet, he later asks me to add another column to indicate whether each character is good or bad.

Some more significant of those characters are

E: *Green Goblin* throws explosive bombs and has a flying skateboard. One day, he almost killed his son, Harry, but *Spider-Man* arrived. He is bad.

Here, the inverted oedipal parricidal phantasy creates a "filicidal" phantasy, seen as the greatest of castrations, but there is already a good part – Spider-Man – that untangles him from this terrifying web.

A: Wow, don't they have feet or hands?
E: It's because their world is full of spikes, and they would die if they got pricked. They either fly with capes, or they have something on their legs that makes them fly, or they have flying cars.

E. continues to explain his fear of castration and of a world he perhaps felt, very early on, to be full of spikes.

E: *Harry* wears a black outfit, and after he discovered that his father was bad, he also became bad, with a costume to kill Spider-Man. He is also bad.
E: The *Hulk* is a good person, but when he has rage attacks, he becomes bad.
A: Angry with what, do you know?
E: I never understand why he gets angry. He is both good and bad.

All these characters are being clarified as internal objects, some malevolent and others more benign, which E. gradually internalizes. He is establishing with more confidence the structuring splits (internal and external, self and other, good and bad, big and small, boys and girls). He is also differentiating generations and genders.

We see the most totalized objects in the last character, Hulk, who is good but has rages, which E. still doesn't fully understand.

He continues his persistent work of investigation and elaboration. He enters and immediately throws himself into drawing. He opens the folder and resumes the drawing of the heroes.

E: There's a country that doesn't have spikes. It's the city of Hulk. Here he doesn't have feet or hands because he came from the city of others where there are spikes.

He draws two more.

E: The *Riddle-Man* has a question mark on his chest. I don't know his real name. But he is bad.
E: The *Mummy* is a mummy.
A: But "mummy" means mother, right?

E. smiles and says that both are written the same way.

Figure 4.24

He flips the sheet and writes, saying,

E: Mummy is for mummy; Mum is for mother, and Mummy is for mama. Dad is for father and Daddy is for papa.

He says affectionately, smiling,

E: You are a Mummy because you are a Mum!

The English spelling of mother and mummy takes us back to ancestral times of origin and the mysteries of life and death, in the famous 'womb-tomb' association. The mother is experienced as a mummy (the dead mother of Green), with the cold and death of transgenerational depression. Transferentially, it seems that I am beginning to differentiate and starting to be experienced by him as a mama, with a life outside of this place, a mother to my children, certainly with a husband, and also being able to fulfill the analytical maternal/paternal function of helping him think.

E. continues:

E: This is the God of Creation; he creates things.
A: Like the mummies and daddies who create babies.
E: There are single mothers.
A: That's true . . . But how do they have their babies?
E: It's the gods.

We are really at the origin, in the time of the creation of the world, of his universe, which he still does not feel as a loving genital union between a mother-woman and a father-man.

In the following session, he enters circumspect. He has a silicone rubber protector in his mouth covering his teeth. Taking it out, he asks me where he can put it, saying it's a protector for rugby. Is he bringing a protector for his sadistic apparatus, to protect me from his furies and from his pulsional invasion? Or is he already capable of transforming violent oral and anal drives within a game with rules, like rugby, which he desired but could not practice? He attentively looks at his last two drawings. E. is silent, which is rare and seems elaborative. The drawing, representing the elaboration at a distance, allows him to think and to continue. E. can look at them and review, now in the elaborative time of the depressive position, through introjective identification and no longer in the acting-out time of the paranoid-schizoid position.

E: You know, I already have the figures from Egypt, this one, this one, and this
     one, showing me in his drawing of the heroes.
A: So your parents have already arrived.
E: Yes. Look, I want to go to the bathroom.

His speech returns to a babyish tone when we touch on the sensitive theme of the trip-separation from his parents.

A: That way you would throw away from me all the poops-and-pee-thoughts that
     scare you, and we couldn't think about them together.
E: Look, if I can't, I'll fart. Take it.

He lets out a loud fart.

A: We're here precisely to see what we do together with these bad smell-thoughts
     that are wandering around your head and you bring here to our consulting room.

Figure 4.25

E. starts to draw.

E: It's a guard; it has a name . . . Help me.
A: Sphinx?
E: Yes. But the drawing, it's not right.

He crumples the paper and throws it in the trash.

We are truly in the times of a very ancient civilization, E. facing both the sphinx, the guardian of destiny, and his history of affiliation. And this fiercely open mouth that he draws tells us of his need to protect us from his sadistic orality (rugby protector).

He picks another sheet and draws again but considers that it's not right either, crumples it, and throws it away.

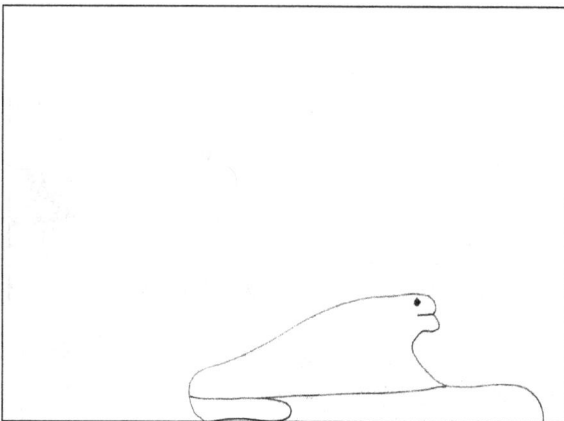

Figure 4.26

E: It's not coming out right.

Here the sphinx is significantly diminished and, just in case, with its mouth shut.
    He draws a snake on another sheet.

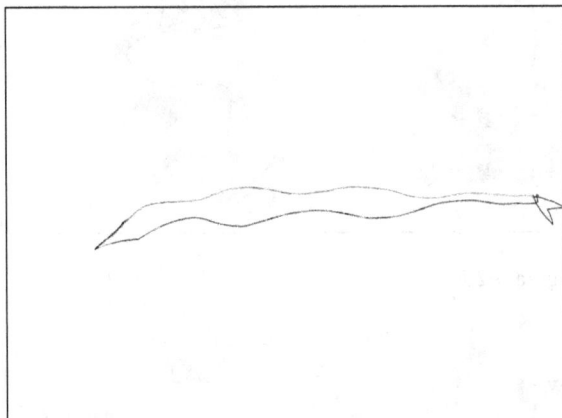

Figure 4.27

E: Akhenaten, their king. It's not right. Argh.

He crumples again the sheet and throws it away.
    This people has a king-snake, a male king, someone feared and the bearer
of the law. E. also has a father, and he will have to identify with him to be
able to make a creative and symbolic use of his qualities, his potency, and his
masculinity.

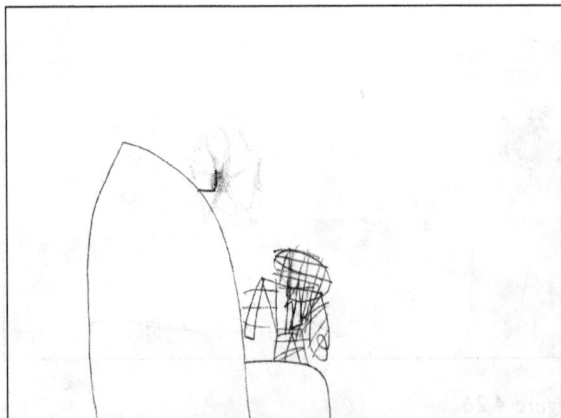

Figure 4.28

He takes that sheet again and on the other side draws a solitary character, caught in webs or mummified, waiting for developments. Him in his difficult crossroads. He also throws it away.

E: Oh . . . I can't do it. I need more sheets. I'm going to use them all, and then what? They are running out. You only give me these sheets; I need many.
A: That way they would all turn into poop-trash.

Following his gesture of drawing on the other side of one of the sheets, I unknead the ones he threw in the trash and place them on the table, turning the blank side up.

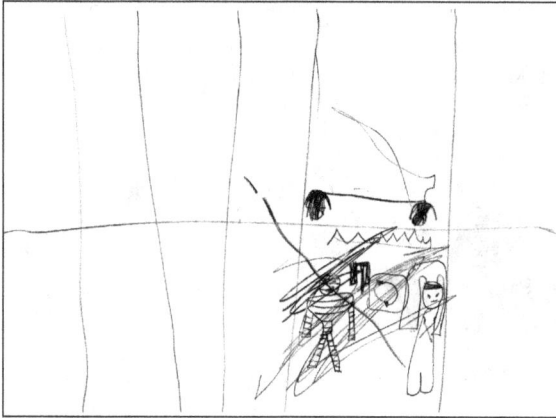

Figure 4.29

He takes the last sheet and draws a grid with some characters and crumples it up and throws it away again, without saying anything about this.

We have here a mummy and a pharaoh. But this mother-mummy and father-pharaoh who were together traveling, distress him, and he does not continue that thought, translating it, as we will see next, into fights.

He takes a used sheet and on the back draws a fight, with the bright and strong colors that usually characterize them. He begins to talk to me while drawing.

Figure 4.30

E: Here is a ladder. I have that fighting game.
A: There are always so many fights in your games, inside you and here between us, aren't there?
E: Yes! Always!
A: Maybe when you can't think of some difficult things.
E: Yes! Take this. (more farts)

Figure 4.31

When he finishes this drawing, he takes another used sheet, and on the back, he draws a "prison-pyramid" with the central part in charcoal pencil and, in contrast, strongly colored on the outside.

A: Do you want to tell me about this?
E: I don't know. I don't know. They are just fights.
A: Well, sometimes it is really difficult for us to understand the fights. Here with me, you are always fighting with the poops, with the sheets that turn into poop, with anger because I don't give you everything you want. And if your drawings go to the trash, do not serve for us to understand together so many struggles.
E: That's it. Just fights. If you gave me more sheets, I would ruin them all.

I associate and dream his drawing, since he does not wish to think/narrate a story: E. mounted on a motorcycle with nondestructive masculine power, with only an eye-mask, but already without a mask, having emerged from his *claustrum*, but sometimes imprisoned in his pyramid-oedipal-triangulation, which demands great internal struggles from him. Struggles with "Sling," as he writes in the drawing, the slingshot that David used to kill Goliath.

He takes the last sheet and draws.

Figure 4.32

E: It's a mummy!

He cuts it out very carefully.

E: Mummies stay inside the?
A: Sarcophagi?!
E: Yes, the sarcophagi. And one day I'm going to Egypt; I've already asked my parents.

At the end of the session, he puts all the drawings in his folder and seems to leave more at ease, knowing that we are containing and working through his struggles, his fecal mummified parts.

Figure 4.32a

This narrative series of eight consecutive drawings, which go from colorless to full of color, returning to the minimalist black and white of the last drawing, clearly portrays the oscillatory movements between the paranoid-schizoid position and the depressive position: the struggles, pulsionally colored, versus the moments when he tries to elaborate on what has been awakened in the last sessions – he facing the sphinx, he facing his origin and his sexuality, he revisiting the characters and ancient fights, more evolved than the first overflowing drawings of partial and destructive drives.

E. now accepts the limit of sheets and accepts using them on the reverse side. He accepts being angry with me without it destroying us, even bringing a teeth protector, just in case. The little mummy he draws last seems to me no longer the Kleinian combined-parent, but now a combined boy-penis-figure which he carefully cuts out and places in his folder. Is it a future reparation possibility of a creator and not a destructive penis? There is a possibility of leaving his dead aspects in a sarcophagus and connecting to life, asking his parents for a visit to Egypt. He, as a child, may be using his parents (in the Winnicottian sense of the use of an object) to expand his knowledge of the world and of himself.

He makes the next series of drawings, entirely in black and white, which is rare. He is more in touch with himself, in a more prevalent depressive position in the Kleinian sense.

At the next session, he enters eager to draw, takes a sheet, and draws a pyramid. On the back, he writes: *Old Times in Egypt.*

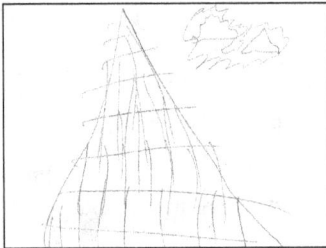

Figure 4.33

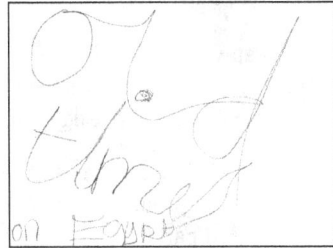

Figure 4.34

He takes another sheet, and while drawing, he speaks.

Figure 4.35

E: Here are some thieves. They stole all the treasure from the pyramid, and a helicopter came; here's the place to take the thieves' bags. This part has no spikes, so this
thief has feet. The one coming from the helicopter also has feet, but here on this
side there are spikes, and when he lands, he will prick himself all over. He's going
to throw a rope to tie all the bags together and have the helicopter pull them.

A: They want to steal all the treasures, but they also are in great danger; either they
end up without feet or prick themselves, and then they can't walk anymore.

E: That's right. That's why some don't have feet or hands. Thus, they will not be
pricked.

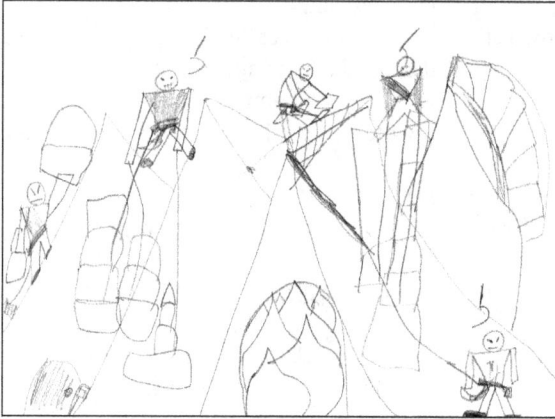

Figure 4.36

Continuing, he then draws the construction of the pyramids with the treasure bags.

E: They are slaves; you see here on top of each one, there are whips. And at this
door (central, full of bags) is the pharaoh. He never appears. They are carrying
huge stones. This one is the strongest. Here, they are building bridges to go
from one to another, see?

Figure 4.37

E. zooms in, starting to draw the interior of the pyramid, with the treasure bags. (See figure 4.37)

A: Here on the wall, there seem to be things written.
E: And there are.
A: What do you think is written there?
E: These are their symbols.
A: They have to organize all those treasures, and they need an alphabet, like you already have learned how to write.
E: I know the Egyptian alphabet, and I bet you don't!
A: What I know is that their letters are called hieroglyphs, and I also know that all peoples needed and created a language to communicate. Like us two here, who have been able to manage to communicate through your drawings.
E: Look, I'm going to draw their signs. This is boy, and here is girl.

But he writes "man" and "girl" on the drawing.
    While he dedicates himself to drawing the Egyptian symbols, he says,

E: Last night, I had a nightmare and called for my dad. I don't remember what it was.

E. continues to reveal his desires to attack the treasures (returning to the theme of the robberies with helicopters) that now belong to the pharaoh, named as king, but who still does not show himself. We already have the door of interdiction to desire, the paternal law. In his pyramidal triangulation in the "Old Times" that Enzo has been organizing phantasmatically, we now have a pharaoh-father, the bags-breasts of maternal/paternal treasure, and a language that begins to structure itself where there are boys and girls in his speech, but still men and girls in the slip of the tongue of his writing in the drawing. He shows more evolved differentiations, with the desires and phantasies of seduction engraved in his inner world, like prehistoric paintings, but now in a growing alpha-betization of his mind. The slaves seem to condense his pregenital or paranoid-schizoid world from the beginning, at different levels of symbolization and integration: his psyche imprisoned in an archaic world; the forced labor of the repetition compulsion; slavery as punishment/castration for incestuous desires; his lack of autonomy and creative freedom due to the difficulty in narcissistically renouncing and evolving to a more humanized and free scenario; and the whip, reminding us of the anal drives of submission. But he also recognizes the dynamism. We have been building bridges to allow for these enslaved parts to circulate in a more symbolized world.
    And at the end is the nightmare. The first verbalized reference to his oneiric world and here also to his possibility of transforming the rawness of his phantasmatic world into dreams. We witness E. constructing his *apparatus* for thinking thoughts, more alpha-betized, through the symbolic representation of the primal scene, the oedipal desires of boys and girls.
    I dreamed within myself the nightmare that E. does not remember: perhaps of not resisting his desire and, in a regressive movement, opening the door and

entering the treasure pyramid to steal it (acting out the originary phantasies), with the consequent retaliatory movements; or perhaps, even more primary, coming into contact with his history and the transgenerational trauma prematurely implicated in it, confusing his functioning. Even if it's a nightmare, it opens the door to dreaming and also opens the possibility for E. to be able to use the treasure of his origin in favor of knowledge (+K), creating a personal language (like the Egyptian writing) in a spontaneous gesture, on his way to his authentic self.

In a session further along, E. arrives fifteen minutes late, which is not usual. The mother, who has been traveling with the father and arrived today, says there was a subway strike. E. speaks in a more childish manner (as he did after Christmas). He resumes a drawing without much willingness. He hears a supposed baby (to me it seems like a cat) crying in the street and says,

E: Oh, this baby is annoying me. Shut up, baby! Ana, tell this damn baby to shut up. Urghhh. . . . How do you write "calda" (syrup)?

He becomes very upset realizing he doesn't know, despite daring to ask.

A: You mean "cauda" (tail)?
E: SHUT UP!!!

He screams loudly and shrill, causing me pain in my ears.

A: It seems to me that you would like to silence the baby inside you and imagine that you are already big and wouldn't need my help to write or even pretend you don't miss our session when you arrive late, or miss your parents when they are traveling. I know it's really hard to be a child and depend on grown-ups. And you get so angry that you wish to enter my ears and hurt me with those screams that really hurt.
E: I really don't need your help!

He spits in my direction. He sings triumphantly and to avoid hearing me, the song of Lady Gaga: *ra ra, uhm ma ma, gaga, u la la.* He repeats the song, and I transform it, singing it with different lyrics.

A: *Boo hoo, uhm, mama, uhm ga ga.* It sounds like the baby's song.
E: Shut up!

He continues singing the song and doodling. At one point, he says,

E: I don't want to draw this anymore.

He puts away the drawing of the heroes.

E. arrives late. He comes in a childish manner as always occurs when there are separations, and the baby he hears crying outside seems to me to be the inner baby that was left without parents, and without me due to his delay, activating the old anxieties of object loss. He gets very angry when faced with his impotence as a seven-year-old boy, who does not know how to write a word (indeed linked to his well-known anality, "tail" as the cord that connects him from behind). We enter again the paranoid-schizoid circuit of narcissistic and sadistic relationship, where E. sees in the mirror his needy, crying baby. I think that the transformation, with humor, of the song *Bad Romance* into the "baby's song" makes some sense for him, which is confirmed by the following change.

E: I thought of a drawing, and I'm going to do it.

For the first time, he "thinks before doing." The thought that, as Bion tells us, allows for linking love and hate, finding a creative outlet. And the drawing thus gains dreamlike qualities of communication, symbolization, and containment of his phantasies, simultaneously reflecting the transferential-countertransferential dynamics.

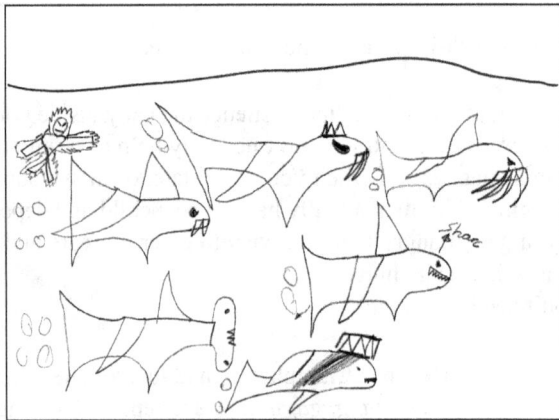

Figure 4.38

E: This line is the sea. Look, I know how to draw sharks; I put this fin like this because they are swimming.
A: I agree that you draw very well for a boy your age. You're beginning to understand your powers and skills as a boy.
E: It's a group of sharks. This is the shark. See if you can guess.
A: No need to guess (I remember the guessing game from the first session) because you clearly drew a hammerhead shark.

E: Here's one that is the chief.

A: It's good that there is a chief. Every group has a chief; otherwise, it would be a big mess, don't you think?

E: Of course! He is the one with the biggest teeth. I'll put a crown on him. There's a smaller one, and I need to draw the queen.

A: And what are these balls?

E: They are the air bubbles from them. And here is a man, the man of the fire. He has a magic that turns into fire, so he can swim with the sharks.

We have a line of the sea in blue, the only minimalist color in the drawing. E., on the threshold of the depressive position, expresses with clarity the still reduced space occupied by external reality compared to the enormous amount of mental space that the phantasies of his inner world still occupy. Phantasies and conflicts, however, are more contained and locatable, inhabitants totalized in a maritime, four-dimensional space, where groups of sharks become differentiated as he draws them. There is the group chief, who deserves a crown; there's a smaller one, and there's a queen, with hair as a feminine attribute, where the sexes seem to be better differentiated. The triangulation is clarified. Sharks of different species can now belong to his group, showing an increasing tolerance toward others. Will it be me the hammerhead shark of his group, different, and always "hammering" him about what he doesn't want to think about?

The bubbles that should come out of the mouth still come out of the tail, a remnant of his well-marked anality from the beginning. And of course, his man-fire-pulsional part, now smaller in size, which can break out at any moment (like the Hulk's fury that he couldn't explain), but who can now swim with the sharks. E. can coexist better with the threatening aspects of his most archaic sadistic phantasies. Gradually, as introjective identifications prevail, he can represent them without being frightened by the concreteness of their persecutory and retaliatory malignancy.

Figure 4.39

Figure 4.40

This last character awakens in me the first drawing of E. in the family (See Figure 4.2), where he was a baby encapsulated in a kind of protective hair.

The hour ends, and he says,

E: Today went by so fast. Let me finish.
A: You can continue in the next session.

While we put the pencils away for him to leave, he says,

E: I'll be back on Thursday.
A: Today is Thursday.
E: Oh, no, on Friday.
A: So you wish you could come back tomorrow? When are you coming back?
E: On Monday, right?

The establishment of the cyclical rhythm of the analytical process – the session, the week, and the weekend – allowed the needy baby to gradually present himself in a more evolved way than at the beginning of the session: enduring the absence of our session time due to his delay; enduring his difficulty as a boy of his age, with the spelling of a word and with the sequence of the days of the week; enduring the waiting for the next session that is not tomorrow; enduring the absence of the object, through greater certainty of his reunion and through the thinkability co-constructed and dreamed together.

Conclusion

E., marked by severe separation anxieties, clearly presented the figurability and narrativity evolution of his emotional landscape through the evolution of his drawings in the analytical process. Drawing became the privileged vehicle for intra and intersubjective communication. He began with undifferentiated scribbles to approach the elaboration of his enigma of the Egyptian/oedipal sphinx.

At the beginning of the analysis, the sessions constituted a phantasmatic stage of overflowing transferential-countertransferential movements of raw experiences in his attempt at oedipal representation and reorganization. The pregenital difficulties, linked to the object separation, the consequent infiltration of disorganizing archaic phantasies, and the acting out of drives without symbolic mediation, plunged him into the world of seduction with its concreteness, subjecting him to cruel anxieties of castration. In the beginning, there was, above all, action and confusion in vain attempts at unsatisfactory plays that, due to symbolic failure, repeatedly fell apart and disorganized, feeding back the cycle of frustration from the repetition compulsion. It is only through figurability/narrativity representation via drawing that Enzo manages to represent these phantasies that are so difficult to translate. Expressed and contained on the sheet of paper, they seem to lose their malignancy and persecutory nature, transforming through *rêverie* and secondary elaboration into a broadening of meanings in creative narratives.

Thus, we witness, in the analytic couple relationship, the progressive and dreamlike unfolding of originary phantasies, organizing themselves into symbolic matrices of drive regulation and the growing alpha function of the mind. By accessing, elaborating, and qualitatively transforming the originary phantasies, Enzo constructed a symbolic matrix that simultaneously allowed him to create and use his *apparatus* for thinking thoughts.

The child drawings taken as the unfolding of a dream, richly depict the movements of the analytical process:

- the dreamlike narrative, the passage from acted nightmare to narrated dream/ story, transformed into a more secondary language
- the co-construction of the container (sheet/room/mind) for the discharge of drives, allowing the progressive alphabetization of the primary process
- the insight of cruel and persecutory emotions, expanding into a more detoxified relational opening
- the permanent working-through of the analytic couple, reflecting the transferential dynamics
- the phantasmatic enactment, allowing for the progressive transformation and creative elaboration of the true self in a potential space

After nine months of analysis, Enzo, already "born" psychically, moves more fluently through the psychic/psychoanalytic spaces: between pleasure and reality (Freud) through imagination; between his paranoid-schizoid and depressive phantasies in a more symbolized object relationship (Klein); by using an object in an expanded transitional-potential space (Winnicott); and by the enlargement of his introjective capability, alpha-betization, or thinkability (Bion) through the *rêverie* of the analytic field.

We witness the enigmatic beauty of a psychoanalytic process, through the permanent updating of the aesthetic conflict (Meltzer).

We are born, so to speak, provisionally anywhere; it is gradually that we compose within ourselves the place of our origin to be born there subsequently each day more definitively.

Rilke – Milan letter of January 23, 1923 (Sztulman, 2004, p. 88)

References

Aberastury, A. (1982). A primeira hora de jogo: seu significado, in Psicanálise da Criança: teoria e técnica. Artes Médicas. pp. 111–134.

Chouvier, B. (2004). Cena Primitiva, in: D. Houzel, M. Emmanuelli, & F. Moggio. (coord.), Dicionário de Psicopatologia da Criança e do Adolescente. Climepsi.

Ferenczi, S. (1913/1992). Um pequeno homem-galo, in: Psicanálise II: obras completas de Sándor Ferenczi, vol. 2., pp. 61–67). Martins Fontes, 1992.

Freud, S. (1911). Formulações sobre os Dois Princípios do Funcionamento Mental, in: Edição Standard Brasileira das Obras Psicológicas Completas de Sigmund Freud, vol. XII. Imago, 1969.

Freud, S. (1917 [1916–17]). Os caminhos da formação dos sintomas, in: Conferências Introdutórias sobre Psicanálise – XXIII, Edição Standard Brasileira das Obras Psicológicas Completas de Sigmund Freud, vol. XVI. Imago, 1976. pp. 419–439.

Geissmann, C. (1995). Les Formes Primitives du Complexe d'OEdipe et le Concept de Névrose Infantile dans la Théorisation Kleinienne et Postkleinienne. Journal de la Psychanalyse de l'Enfant, 17. Bayard.

Green, A. (2000). Experience and Thinking in Analytic Practice, in: J. Abram (ed.), André Green at the Squiggle Foundation. Karnac.

Hinshelwood, R.D. (1992). Dicionário do Pensamento Kleiniano. Artes Médicas.

Houzel, D., Emmanuelli, M. & Moggio, F. (coord.) (2004). Dicionário de Psicopatologia da Criança e do Adolescente. Climepsi.

Klein, M. (1926). Princípios Psicológicos da Análise de Crianças Pequenas, in: Amor, Culpa e Reparação e outros trabalhos (1921–1945), vol. I Obras Completas de Melanie Klein. Imago, 1996.

Klein, M. (1928). Estágios Iniciais do Conflito Edipiano, in: A Psicanálise de Crianças, vol. II Obras Completas de Melanie Klein. Imago, 1997.

Klein, M. (1929). Personificações no Brincar das Crianças, in: Amor, Culpa e Reparação e outros trabalhos (1921–1945), vol. I Obras Completas de Melanie Klein. Imago, 1996.

Klein, M. (1930). A Importância da Formação de Símbolos no Desenvolvimento do Ego, in: Amor, Culpa e Reparação e outros trabalhos (1921–1945), vol. I Obras Completas de Melanie Klein. Imago, 1996.

Klein, M. (1945). O Complexo de Édipo à luz das ansiedades arcaicas, in: Amor, Culpa e Reparação e outros trabalhos (1921–1945), vol. I Obras Completas de Melanie Klein. Imago, 1996.

Laplanche, J. & Pontalis, J.-B. (1986). Vocabulário da Psicanálise. 9ª ed. Martins Fontes.

Laplanche, J. & Pontalis, J.-B. (1988). Fantasia Originária, Fantasias das Origens, Origens da Fantasia. Zahar.

Meltzer, D. (1967). The Psycho-Analytical Process. Clunie Press, 1990.

Perron-Borelli, M. (1997). Dynamique du Fantasme. PUF.

Silva, A. & Santos, L. (1995). As últimas cartas do Agostinho . . . Org. de Luís dos Santos. Edição da Cooperativa de Animação Cultural de Alhos Vedors. Carta I, p. 3. (http://arquivo.ese.ips.pt/ese/destaques/agsilva/cartas%20agostinho.pdf).

Sverdlik, M. (2010). La creación del pensamiento en los orígines: estudio psicoanalítico acerca de las fantasías y teorías sexuales infantiles. Teseo.

Sztulman, H. (2004). Arcaico, in: D. Houzel, M. Emmanuelli, & F. Moggio (coord.), Dicionário de Psicopatologia da Criança e do Adolescente. Climepsi, 2000.

About confidentiality

Raquel Quelhas Lima

The commitment to confidentiality that psychoanalysts guarantee to their analysands is a matter of respect for their privacy and a mandatory condition for free association, the fundamental rule of psychoanalysis. However, the disclosure of clinical material in communications or publications is important and desirable for the ongoing training of psychoanalysts, whose ultimate benefit will be that of the patients themselves.

The debate on this dilemma began with Sigmund Freud, in his introduction (pp. 6-8) to Dora's case (1905), in which he argued that the conflict is insoluble, but it is necessary to favour the search for truth, science, in the name of the ethics of psychoanalysis.

The various contributions on how to reconcile these two needs result in the obligation to conceal identity and disguise clinical material, among the various systematized by Gabbard (2000) thick disguise, patient consent, process approach, use of composite materials, and use of a colleague as the author.

As two of us (Isabel Quinta da Costa and Raquel Quelhas Lima) had the opportunity to defend at the Psychoanalysis Forum on Confidentiality, organized by the Portuguese Psychoanalytical Society in January 2017, we consider that informed consent is not applicable in the case of analyses with children and adolescents. Consent would have to be given by the parents, both because they themselves are also involved and also because the children are minors. However, this consent could be challenged by them in the future. The consent given by the parents would also imply a breach of confidentiality regarding what goes on in the sessions, which we don't consider acceptable. Parents' natural interest and concern for their children, as well as the usual inclusion of sessions with parents in psychoanalytic work with children, should not be confused with the "right to know" invoked by some and which, in our opinion, mainly shows a need for control that reveals difficulties in differentiation that are blocking children's development.

For this book, we have reflected extensively on various contributions in the current discussion on this delicate subject and have resorted to the methods considered most appropriate for each case.

DOI: 10.4324/9781003584018-6

References

Freud, S. (1905). Fragment of an Analysis of a Case of Hysteria (1905[1901]). The Standard Edition of the Complete Psychological Works of Sigmund Freud, Volume VII (1901-1905): A Case of Hysteria, Three Essays on Sexuality and Other Works, pp. 1–122.

Gabbard, G.O. (2000). Disguise or Consent: Problems and Recommendations Concerning the Publication and Presentation of Clinical Material. *The International Journal of Psychoanalysis*, 81(6): 1071–1086.

Biographical notes

Ana Belchior Melícias

Ana Belchior Melícias was born in Luanda-Angola. She graduated in Clinical Psychology and specialized in Psychoanalysis at Sedes Sapientiæ in São Paulo-Brazil. In Lisbon-Portugal, she became member of the Portuguese Psychoanalytical Society (PPS) and of the International Psychoanalytical Association (IPA). She is a Child and Adolescent psychoanalyst (COCAP) and won the Accésit of the Second Edition of the Rebeca Grinberg Award (2019) from Madrid Psychoanalytical Association. She is trainer at the PPS Institute of Psychoanalysis and of the Bick method. She is a member of the Association Internationale pour le Développement de l'Observation du Bébé selon Bick and Founder and President of the APOBB (Portuguese Association of Infant Observation Bick). Institutionally she has collaborated in several positions and more recently was vice president of the PPS board (2022–2023) and was nominated by Harriet Wolfe (IPA President) as member of the Lisbon Local Arrangements Committee for the 54th IPA Congress (2025).

She divides her activity between private practice with infants/families, children, adolescents, and adults, and teaching both in academic scope and linked to psychoanalytic training. She regularly presents scientific papers, many of them published in several national and international journals in Portuguese, English, German, Spanish, Catalan, and Polish. She is an author in books including *Colonialism: between Psychoanalysis and Art; Paula Rego: Psychoanalytical Essays; Psychoanalysis & Cinema: Dialogues; Psicanalisarium: Four Children on the Couch* (2nd ed.); *Infant Observation: Method and Applications; Sigmund Freud 150 Years Later; The Freud Folder* in English, Portuguese, and Spanish; *Mind in the Line of Fire: Psychoanalytic Voices to the Challenges of Our Time/Mente en la línea de fuego: voces psicoanalíticas ante los retos de nuestro tiempo*; and the *Timeline of the Portuguese Psychoanalytical Society* (3rd ed.).

She is currently Editorial Advisor of the *Annual Book of Psychoanalysis* (Brazil) – *International Journal of Psycho-Analysis* and is part of the Scientific Board of the *German Yearbook for Child and Adolescent Psychoanalysis* (Munich). She has co-founded and is co-editor of the Cinema & Psychoanalysis Blog, and is the editor of the Freud & Companhia Publishing House.

Isabel Quinta da Costa

Isabel Quinta da Costa is a psychoanalyst member of the Portuguese Psychoanalytical Society (PPS), with additional training in Child and Adolescent Psychoanalysis (COCAP). She is also member of the European Federation of Psychoanalysis and the International Psychoanalytical Association.

At the Department of Child Psychiatry at Maria Pia Hospital, she was part of the outpatient consultation team for twenty years, focusing on prevention and intervention within the mother–infant dyad and on working with children suffering from severe developmental problems through balneotherapy. She also worked as a group psychotherapist (free play and painting) with latency-stage children and conducted psychodrama sessions with adolescents.

Within the Portuguese Psychoanalytic Society, she held leadership, organizational, and training roles for four years in external training courses.

Since 2022, she has held leadership and psychoanalytic training roles at the Institute of Psychoanalysis in Porto.

As a psychodramatist and full member of the Portuguese Society of Psychoanalytic Group Psychodrama, she also contributes to training candidates.

Currently, she conducts clinical work in private practice with children and their families as well as with adolescents and adults. She is a clinical supervisor for cases involving children in psychotherapy or psychoanalysis.

Elsa Couchinho

Elsa Couchinho is a clinical psychologist who graduated from the Instituto Superior de Psicologia Aplicada (Lisbon). She is member of the Portuguese Psychoanalytical Society (PPS) and a Child and Adolescent psychoanalyst (COCAP). She is a member of the International Psychoanalytical Association and the European Federation of Psychoanalysis.

Couchinho has also served as a trainer at the Institute of Psychoanalysis (Lisbon) in clinical, adolescent, and psychosis seminars, and COCAP (Committee for Child and Adolescent Psychoanalysis) training.

She conducts her private practice in Lisbon. Alongside her clinical work, she has several participations in intervention projects with children, adolescents, and families from vulnerable populations, demonstrating a special interest in the applicability of psychoanalytic thought. She co-founded the outreach group "Cinema & Psychoanalysis" and the blog "Cinema & Psychoanalysis." She supervises multidisciplinary teams in the context of residential homes for children and youth at risk, and at the Dr. João dos Santos Center.

Raquel Quelhas Lima

Raquel Quelhas Lima is a child and adolescent psychiatrist and psychoanalyst, a member of the Portuguese Psychoanalytical Society (PPS) and of the Institute for

Psychoanalytic Training and Therapeutics of Porto (IFTP), with additional training in Child and Adolescent Psychoanalysis (COCAP), member of the International Psychoanalytical Association and of the Fédération Européenne de Psychanalyse.

During the period of hospital activity, the author emphasizes articulation with primary health care in the promotion of child and youth mental health and child psychiatry liaison work in a global and globalizing psychosomatic approach.

She currently develops her clinical activity only in the private practice by doing psychotherapy and psychoanalysis with children, adolescents, and adults and also does clinical supervision work.

In the PPS and IFTP, she has had training, organizational, and directive functions (in the board of PPS and IFTP) and served on the Ethics Committee.

Currently, she is president of IFTP and is part of the board and of the Training Committee of PPS.

She is the author and co-author of several communications and publications in the field of clinical and research in child psychiatry and psychoanalysis.

Index

Note: Page numbers in *italics* indicate a figure and page numbers in **bold** indicate a table on the corresponding page.

Aberastury, Arminda 3
Abraham, Karl 2
actions, dictation 33
adults: sexuality, traumatic intrusion 60; voice/manner, granddaughter imitation 20
affective disconnection, mother absence 4
affiliation, history 89
aggressive phantasy, confusion 69
aggressivitiy: consequences, fear 47; increase 57
Aichhorn, August 2
airplane-penis, castration threat 78–79, *77–78*
Alfred-Binet Center 3
alone, feeling 10
alpha-betization 96
alpha function 82; beta elements, progressive transformation 85
anaclitic depression, concept (introduction) 2–3
anal castration 73
anality 99
anal phantasies, eroticization 73
anal sadistic phantasies 60
anal-urethral state 65
analysis *see* psychoanalysis
analytical process, cyclical rhythm (establishment) 100
analytic couple relationship 101
analytic field, co-constructions 4
anger (parents) 31
annihilation, dimension 47
appointment: grandmother request 6; scheduling 6–7

archaic phantasies, profusion 74
archaic sadistic phantasies: impact 65; threatening aspects, coexistence 99, *99*
asthma, development 9
autoerotic rhythmic movements 43
autonomy, desire 11
awakening onset 35–36

babies, hunger 40
babyish speech 65–66
baby-poop, display 64, 66, 73
baby, protective hair (encapsulation) *99*, 100
bad guys: attack 52; pursuit 36
bad objects, emergence 35
beta elements, progressive transformation 85
Bick, Esther 3
Bionian School 3
Bion, Wilfred Ruprecht 3
birthing experience 63
blessed, arrival 29
body (transformation), incubator (symbol) 23
boo-boos, witnessing 34
boundaries, establishment 6
Bowlby, John 3
boy-penis-figure 94
braces: drawings *8*; pain, discussion 7–8; symbolic perspective 8
breast–feces–penis–babies–money axis 61
breastfeeding: interruption 40; intimacy 43
breast, loss 74
breast–penis–babies–money (maternal body, Christmas police protection) *79*, 79
butt, kiss (drawing) 72–73, *72*

calmness, mother continuation 54
castration 86; airplane-penis, castration
    threat *77–78*, 78–79; anal castration
    73; anxiety 47; fear, explanation 86;
    phantasy 59–61, 74
cheating, usage 46, 48
childhood: omnipotence, surrender 56;
    trauma 68
child-in-the-family 4
child psychoanalysis: description 4–5;
    impact 2
children: cross-identification, dynamics
    (balance) 32; psyche, adult sexuality
    (traumatic intrusion) 60
Christmas police, gift protection *79*, 79
circles of hell: Oedipus 37; wicked/witches,
    residence 36
classmates: aggression, display 30;
    interactions, problems 13
claustrum: emergence 93; maternal body
    claustrum 73
closeness, regressive desire 43
Clown-Lady-mother, presentation 80, *81*
Clown-Lady, police arrest 80, *80*
collaboration possibility, increase 81
Committee for Children and Adolescent
    Psychoanalysis (COCAP) 2
communication: Bionian sense 73;
    dreamlike qualities 98
companionship, providing 30
competitive games, invention 56–57
conception (birth)/filiation (symbolic fact),
    conjunction 60
confidentiality, commitment 103
contradictions/differences, fertility 1
convergence, advocacy 1
cooperation-repair, landscape (visit) 81
correlative seduction 60
countertransference feeling, support 6
countertransferential elements,
    motivation 38
creative/enriching movement, struggle 82
creative outlet, search 98
cross-identification, dynamics (balance) 32
cruelty, effects 75

daddy, word (drawing) *87*, 87–88
dance, granddaughter exploration 27
Dante Alighieri 29; work, association
    29–30
daydreaming, space (creation) 85
death: destruction-death 76; drive
    (Thanatos) 3, 35; risk, experience 50

decisive reality, psychic reality
    (equivalence) 62
defense mechanisms 34
depression: family history 40;
    transgenerational depression 88
depressive/abandonment anxieties,
    emergence 26
depressive position 94; elaborative time 88;
    schizo-paranoid position, dynamic 38;
    threshold 99
destruction-death 76
destructive attacks, identification 35
destructiveness: effects 75; interpretation
    35; occurrence 30
destructive penis 94
Diatkine, René 3
difficulties, display 31
disguise 9
disheveled disjointed child,
    representation 31
disruptions, source 74
dissociation, representation 33
distance, feelings (granddaughter
    processing) 15
distrust 7
Divine Comedy, The (Dante) 29, 38
Dolto, Françoise 3
dominance/submission, movements 73
drawings (link), therapeutic alliance
    (drawings symbolization) 43
dream-for-two, transformation 1
dreaming 35–38
dreamless sleep, death (envelopment) 33
dreams: boundaries 35–36; recall, inability
    36; unfolding 101
dress, analyst self-observation 38

earth, human existence (unfolding) 30
Ego Psychology 3
Egyptian symbols (hieroglyphs), drawing
    95, 96
elaborative drawing 88
elementary school, granddaughter
    transition 24
emotional experience, figurability/
    narrativity 61
emotions: absence 33; disorganization 74
Enzo (E): all my lego, drawing *87*; babyish
    speech 65–66; baby-poop, display
    64, 66, 73; butt, kiss (drawing) *72*,
    73; Christmas holiday, separation
    (experience) 78, *79*; Christmas police,
    gift protection *79*, 79; crying intensity,

reduction 67; differentiations 96;
distress/disconnection, feeling 71;
Egyptian symbols (hieroglyphs),
drawing 95, 96; elaborative drawing
88; Enzo-poop, presentation 64;
epistemophilic instinct, Riddler-Enzo
representation 80; father, drawing
65–66, 65; father/son, drawing 77;
feeling, forbidding 61–62; first session
62–67; games 63–64; guessing game
63–64; Harry Potter drawing 83,
83–84; hero drawings 85, 85–86,
97; hero drawings, continuation 87;
immediate gratification, tolerance 86;
initial sessions 62; king-snake (male
king), drawing 90, 90–91; maternal/
paternal lineage, story (drawing) 77,
77; monster-heroes, differentiation
(absence) 76, 76; mother, nakedness
(drawing) , 73; mother/pee-pee drawing
64–65, 65; name, writing (difficulties/
gap) 64; narrative, enactment
(problem) 68; object loss 68; origin,
phantasmatization 64; parents (trip
separation), speech (change) 88; partial/
incomplete object, drawing 69–70, 70;
patient, case study 61; peeing/pooping,
drawing 71, 71; phantasmatic organizing
96; play 64, 69; poop-trash, conversion
91; pregenital confusion, translation 65;
primary maternal-analytical concern 64;
prison-pyramid 92, 92–93; pyramidal
triangulation 96; regressed state 68;
rêverie, usage 64; rocket, drawing 71,
72; sadistic primal scene, regressive
return 81, 81–82; screaming 66, 97;
second session 66–70; self-portrait
69–70; separation, anxieties 68;
sharks, drawing 98, 98–99; singing
97; slingshot, drawing 92, 93; sphinx,
drawing 89, 89; spitting 97; summer
vacation 71; third session 68–70;
tiny books, creation 74–75, 75; truth,
hearing 63
epistemophilic instinct, Riddler-Enzo
representation 80
Eros (life drive) 3, 35
eroticization 73
European Federation of Psychoanalysis 2
expulsion, phantasy 59

family: analyst, alliance 32; conflict,
intensification 11; depression, history
40; interaction 31–32; myth 79; suicide
attempts, history 40; therapies 5
family-in-the-child (transgenerationality) 4
fantasy: boundaries 35–36; absence
38; oral incorporation, cannibalistic
fantasies 44; originary phantasies,
symbolic matrix 59; phantasies, types
59–60
father: assistance, increase (expectation)
12; ears, growth (drawing) 65, 65;
exhaustion, feeling 10; idealization,
patient surrender 56; intervention
17; knife attack 84; Ninja father,
drawing 77, 78; perceptiveness 17;
pharaoh-father 96; police-father,
protection (internalization) 79;
preferential relationship 40; presence
41; presence/activity, increase 17;
self-confidence, increase 48
father-pharaoh 91, 91
feces: phallus, confounding 47;
representation, marbles (usage) 48;
retention 54
feelings, verbalization 49
Ferenczi, Sándor 2
fighting game 92, 93
filiation, symbolic fact 60
filicidal phantasy 86
Flora (F): analyst description 32; calm,
return 32; internal realm, bad objects
(presence) 35; patient case study 30–31;
sleep 34–35; witness, role (assumption)
34; wounds, analyst remedies 34
forest, symbolization 37
Fort-Da, observation 2
French School (Lacanian School) 3
Freud, Anna 2; technique, Klein technique
(antagonism) 3–4
Freud, Sigmund 103; concepts,
deepening/expansion 3; Hans, visit 2;
incorporation/expulsion, phantasies 59;
psychic functioning, complementarity
nature 4; psychic reality, decisive
reality (equivalence) 62; "Two
Principles" 85
future, dreaming 38

games: maintenance 49; repetition 44–45;
transitional object function 50
geographic confusion, appearance 73
gestures, dictation 33
ghost a thousand ghosts, playing 45
ghosts 40

grandmother: clinic presence, announcement (absence) 11; daughter complaints 10; daughter issue 11; demands, resistance 28; manipulation 9
Green Goblin: bomb throwing 85, 86; son (drawing) 83, 84
guessing game 63–64
guiding thread (*fil rouge*) 1

Hagrid 83, 83; benevolence 85
Harry Potter: badness, discovery 85, 86
Harry Potter drawing 83, 83–84
Hat Man, drawing 83, 83
hell circles, wicked/witches (residence) 36
Hell, patient traversal 30
helplessness, feeling 10
hero drawings 85, 85–86, 97; continuation 87
hide-and-seek game, usage 44
home: bedroom changes 22; description/drawing 14–15; valuable objects, presence 15
hope, nourishment 82
horror, experience 33
hospitalism, concept (introduction) 2–3
houses (game), play 56
hug-Hellmuth, Hermine von 2
Hulk, rage attacks (badness) 85, 86, 99
humanization, anticipation 76
human limitations, acceptance 29

idealized parental couple, representation (emergence) 36
identity-clothing 85, 85–86
illusion, transformation 6
imagination, space (creation) 85
immediate gratification, tolerance 86
incestuous desires, punishment/castration 96
inconsolable outbursts (experience), cause (absence) 30
incorporation, phantasy 59
incubator: granddaughter description/drawing 22–23, 23; metaphor 23
infantile sexual theories, framework 61
initial encounters, reflection 37
inner self, experiences (integration) 25
integration, advocacy 1
interdiction, door 96
intergenerational hierarchy, confusion 7
internal cohesion, increase 25
internal conflicts, locating/containing 84

internal objects: clarification 86; disconnection 33; interiorization 41; stabilization 36
International Psychoanalytical Association (IPA) 2
intrauterine life, phantasy 59
introjective identifications 99
intrusive identification 60
inverted oedipal parricidal phantasy 86

jewelry, analyst self-observation 38
joint sleepover, intimacy (representation) 35
Joker: drawing 82, 82; police arrest 79, 80
Joker-father 80, 81

king-snake (male king), drawing 90, 90–91
Kleinian School 3
Klein, Melanie 2, 35; technique, Freud technique (antagonism) 3–4

Lacan, Jacques 3
ladder (drawing) 92, 93
Lebovici, Serge 3
life drive (Eros) 3, 35
lineage, phantasies 77
loneliness, feelings (granddaughter processing) 15
love: connection/quality, awareness (growth) 80; mental health axis 62
ludic material, interest (absence) 40

magic, existence (question) 66
Mahler, Margaret 3
malignancy, concreteness 99
manic defenses, usage 62
marital relationship, cooling 62
masculine identity, reinforcement 47
maternal body: breast–penis–babies–money, Christmas police protection 79; claustrum 73; plundering 73
maternal/paternal treasure, bags-breasts 96
maternal territory, treasure (intrusive thefts) 84
math, doing (enjoyment) 52
Meltzer, Donald 3
menstruation, information (need) 25
mentalization, capacity (increase) 58
mental space 99
Middle Group (Independent Group) 3
mind: alpha-betization 96; alpha function 82

mirror, psychoanalyst role 36
monster, being (desire) 52–54
monster-heroes, differentiation (absence) 76, *76*
Morgenstern, Sophie 2
mother: absence/affective disconnection 41; breast, relationship 43; calmness, continuation 54; changes, unacceptance 16; Clown-Lady-mother, presentation 80, *81*; depression 62; devaluation/exclusion, feeling 16; grandmother issue 11; manipulation 9; meeting, scheduling 25; nakedness, drawing 72, *72*; power, psychoanalyst power (comparison) 46; Rita accusations 7; Rita argument 11; Rita complaints 9; role, failure (feeling) 6–7; terminal illness, diagnosis 10; toilet-mother, role 76
mother-infant psychotherapies 5
mother-mummy 91, *91*
Mother Nature, representation 37
mother-room-body protection 73
mourning, trauma 60
mouse, granddaughter discussion/drawing 23–24, *23*
Mummy *85*, 87
mum, word (drawing) 87–88, *88*

nameless terror 33
narcissistic failures, elaboration 60–61
narcissistic lack 74
narcissistic traumas 60
narration, forms 61
narrative, enactment (attempt) 68
near-death experience, horror 33
nightmares 96; horror, patient display 33
Ninja father, drawing *77*, *78*
nondestructive masculine power 92
numbers (writing), interest (growth) 52

object: loss 68; progressive internalization 28
oedipal conflict: axis 61; castration phantasy 74; component phantasy 75; parricidal phantasy 78
oedipal drama, phantasmatic trilogy 59
oedipal themes, emergence (mental space) 38
oedipal triad, representation 80, *81*
Oedipus (circle of hell) 37
Oedipus, primal scene 60
Old Times in Egypt 94; events *94–95*

oral incorporation, cannibalistic fantasies 44
oral phantasies, eroticization 73
oral sadistic phantasies 60
origin: facing 94; myth 79; phantasmatization 64
originary phantasies: link, potential 60; symbolic matrix 59
originary (Ur), representation possibility (absence) 61
originary schemes, encounter 61

pain, soothing 62
paper fortune-teller, creation 9
Paradise, blessed (arrival) 29
paranoid-schizoid position: movements 73; oscillatory movements 94
paranoid-schizoid world, condensation 96
parents: abilities, insecurity reinforcement (avoidance) 41; anger 31; childhood experiences, connection 31; childhoods, separations (trauma) 68; cross-identification, dynamics (balance) 32; flexibility 25; idealized parental couple, representation (emergence) 36; informing, obligation 6; interview 9; love (connection/quality), awareness (growth) 80; meeting, daughter reaction 25; qualities/abilities, daughter description 14; relationship, understanding 41; session, teacher compliments (mentioning) 52; shortcomings, perception 31–32; trip separation, speech (change) 88
parricidal phantasy 59, 78; inverted oedipal parricidal phantasy 86
parricidal wish 84; retaliation 78
parricide, oedipal conflict (component phantasy) 75
paternal figure, patient search 45
paternal function, limits setting 73
paternal grandmother, death 10
patient psyche, psychoanalyst exploration 34
pencil, phallic symbol 54
perfection realm, princess inhabitation 36
persecutory/retaliatory malignancy, concreteness 99
Peter (P): aggressiveness 46; aggressivity, consequences (fear) 47; aggressivity, increase 57; annihilation, dimension 47; ants, drawing 50; autoerotic rhythmic

movements 43; baby, playing 44; bad day, perception 54–55; castration anxiety 47; cheating, usage 46, 48; childhood omnipotence, surrender 56; circles, drawing 50; competitive games, invention 56–57; death, risk (experience) 50; dilemma 57; drawings (link), therapeutic alliance (drawings symbolization) 43; eat/drink/sleep, growth (poisonous perception) 53; erotic aspects 47; father idealization, surrender 56; feces, phallus (confounding) 47; feces, retention 54; feelings, verbalization 49; filth, deletion 49; fury 49; "Gangnam Style" (singing) 47; ghost a thousand ghosts, playing 45; hate, expression 58; hide-and-seek game, usage 44; houses (game), play 56; laughter (satisfaction) 44; masculine identity, reinforcement 47; math, doing (enjoyment) 52; monster, being (desire) 52–53; mother presence, feeling 42; movement, repetition 42; numbers (writing), interest (growth) 52; oral incorporation, cannibalistic fantasies 44; paternal figure, search 45; patient case study 40; pencil (phallic symbol) 54; penguin, transformation 56; plaque, drawing 55, 55; potency, money symbolization 47; powers, playing 52; progressive integration process (allowance) 49–50; proposals, refusal 40; pullover/psychic envelope 42; regressive behavior, satisfaction 43; runaway ball game, usage 44; scribbles 42, 50–51; secretions, retention 54; self-confidence, increase 48; self-strengthening, master/analyst (impact) 55; session, absences 49; session, cancellations 57; session, father attendance (result) 42; sister, equivalence (desire) 57–58; sister, monster (equivalence) 53; sleepwalker, pretending 53; small animal game 57; small penis, drawing 46, 46–47; space, notion i(experience) 50; strength, symbolic expression 57; suicide, threat 45; toilet usage, fear 47; Twin Towers, consideration 55; walking cactus/man drawing 51; weapons list, repetition 55; wheels/breasts, highlighting/drawing 43, 43; writing 54

Peter (P), games: maintenance 49; repetition 44–45; transactional object function 50
Peter Parker (Spider-Man) 83, 84
phallic phantasies, eroticization 73
phantasies: containment 98–99; destructive level 74; forms 61; reality, distinction 85; symbolic matrices presentation 61; types 59–60; unfolding 101
phantasmatic organizing 96
phantasmatic trilogy, psychic organization 60
pharaoh-father 106
play scenario 68
pleasure: exclamations 43; principle, transition 85
pluralism, richness 1
plush dolls, games (maintenance) 49
police-father, protection (internalization) 79
poop-thoughts, metabolization 73
poop-trash, conversion 91
Portuguese Psychoanalytical Society 2, 103
postpartum depression 10; symptoms 40
potency, money symbolization 47
powers (game), playing 52
pregenital confusion, translation 65
pregenital world, condensation 96
pre-oedipal loss, experiences (inheritance) 61
pre-oedipal tone, channeling 71
primal scene: evocation 74; human terms representations 81; phantasy 59, 61; sadistic primal scene, regressive return 81, 81–82; vitalization 77
primary maternal-analytical concern 64
primary phantasies, realm 68
primary process, secondarization 85
primitive beta elements, emergence 73
prison-pyramid 92, 92–93
progress, idealization (representation) 30
progressive integration process (allowance) 49
progressive/regressive movements, dynamism 82
projective identification 2, 60
provocations, increase 45
psychic distress, witness 34
psychic envelope, creation 84
psychic functioning 35; complementarity nature 4
psychic life, organizers (identification) 2–3

psychic organization: fragility 69;
simultaneous levels 4
psychic reality, decisive reality
(equivalence) 62
psychic suffering: destruction/damage/
annihilation 34; torments, occurrence
29–30
psychoanalysis: frequency, continuation
58; importance 6; proposal 41; sessions
(marking), calendar (usage) 26
Psychoanalysis Forum on
Confidentiality 103
psychoanalyst: anger, patient perception/
interpretation 47; container function
42; control 33; drowsiness 32–34;
mirror role 36; object, reduction 33;
power, mother power (comparison) 46;
projection 37; sleep, description 33
psychoanalytical process, analytical couple
(functioning) 61
psychoanalytic-inspired psychotherapies 5
psychoanalytic psychotherapy,
commencement 30–31
psychoanalytic reflection 60
psychoanalytic treatment, proposal 31
psychosexuality (processing), time/space
(granddaughter usage) 24
psychotherapy, course of action 30
psychotic defense mechanisms,
understanding (broadening) 33
pullover/psychic envelope 42
pulsional dialectic, focus 3
punishment, fear 229
Purgatory, patient traversal 30
pyramid: interior, drawing 95, 96
pyramidal triangulation 96
pyramid, drawings 94–95, 95
pyramid-oedipal-triangulation,
imprisonment 92

Rambert, Madeleine 2
reality: boundaries 35–36; boundaries,
absence 38; principle, approach 85
regressive behavior, satisfaction 43
relationship, containment 65
retention/expulsion, movements 73
rêverie: resilience/capacity, testing 73–74;
usage 64
Riddle-Man, badness 85, 87
Riddler: epistemophilic instinct,
Riddler-Enzo representation 80, 80;
police arrest 79, 80

Rita (R): adult voice/manner imitation 20;
autonomy, testing 16; babies, drawing
13, 14, 21, 23; bedroom changes 22;
braces, discussion 7–8, 22; braces,
discussion/drawing 7–8, 8; braces,
drawings 8; Brazilian bracelets/wishes,
discussion 20; chameleon, drawing
8, 8; change, sign (appearance) 26;
cleanliness habits, mother worry 25;
dance, exploration 27; depressive/
abandonment anxieties, emergence 26;
disappointments, absence 16; distance,
increase 20; distance/loneliness,
feelings (processing) 15; end-of-year
exam preparation 19; end-of-year
party, discussion 20; excitement,
drive-related origin 24; exclusion/
abandonment, feeling/drawing 18–19,
18; farm events 24; grandmother
criticism 6; green girl, drawing 19–20,
19; holiday memories, revisit 24;
home, description/drawing 14–16, 15;
homework (completion), assistance
(absence) 16–17; incubator, description/
drawing 22–23, 23; irritation, mother
complaints (impact) 18; liquid glue,
usage/results 24, 25–26; masturbation,
hint 27; mother, argument 11; parental
abandonment/care absence 21; patient
case study 30; physical changes 26;
psychosexuality (processing), time/
space usage 24; punishment, fear 27;
secret, sharing 17–20; separation
tolerance, increase 26; sin, fear 27;
sky/tree/steps taking, drawing 26, 26;
smart mouse, discussion/drawing 24,
23; story elements, drawing 17, 18–19;
success, absence 10–11; sunflower
drawing 12, 12; traffic light, drawing
27; upside-down world, drawing 27, 29;
vacation, enjoyment 22
Rita (R) at school: anxiety 24;
attention-seeking behaviors 24;
classmaters, closeness/identification
27; integration/enjoyment 24;
responsibility 20
rooster, crow (sound) 35
royal road (dreams) 4
runaway ball game, usage 44

sadism, occurrence 29–30
sadistic orality, protection 89

sadistic phantasies 60; confusion 68;
    eroticization 73
sadistic primal scene, regressive return
    81, 81
Santos, João dos 4
schizo-paranoid position: defense
    mechanism characteristic 34; depressive
    position, dynamic 38; frustration/
    discomfort, experience 35
school: anxiety 24; attention-seeking
    behaviors 24; daughter, crying 11;
    group, nonintegration 11; integration/
    enjoyment 24
scribbles/scribbling 42, *50–51*, 59;
    drawing, expression 69
secondary school, granddaughter entry 24
secretions, retention 54
seduction: phantasy 59, 60; world 100
self: annihilation, frustration/discomfort
    (experience) 35; gradual de-idealization
    37; partial representation 37; sense,
    imprisonment 8
Self Psychology 3
sensoriality, immersion 29
separation: anxieties 100; experiences,
    inheritance 61, 74; granddaughter
    tolerance, increase 26; pain 64, 73;
    trauma 60
separation/individuation process,
    difficulty 10
sexes, difference (origin) 59
sexuality: facing 94; origin 59
sharks, drawing *98*, 98–99
siblinghood 2
siblings: competition 7; granddaughter
    enjoyment 22; interactions, problems 12
sin, fear 27
sister: monster, equivalence 53; patient
    equivalence, desire 57
slavery, punishment/castration 96
slingshot, drawing 92, *93*
smell-thoughts 88–89
Sokolnicka, Eugénie 2
son-in-law, grandmother criticism 6
Soulé, Michel 3
space: abstract notions 50; mental space
    99; notion, experience 50; organization,
    vertical lines (usage) 77; reduction
    99–99
speech, dictation 33
sphinx: drawing 89, *89*; diminishment 90;
    facing 94

Spider-Man (Peter Parker) *83*, 84; web,
    disentanglement *85*, 86
Spitz, René 2
strength, symbolic expression 57
structuring splits, establishment 86
student, teacher (concerns) 10
suicide: attempts, family history 40; patient
    threat 45
symbolic equivalents, chain 74
symbolic failure 74, 100
symbolic matrix 59; construction 101;
    presentation 61
symbolization: access 41; dreamlike
    qualities 98; failure, display 69;
    progressive possibility 40

teacher: complaint 10; compliments,
    parents (mentioning) 52;
    concerns 11
Thanatos (death drive) 3, 35
theoretical-clinical trajectory,
    evidence 4
therapeutic relationship, incubator
    (metaphor) 23
thinking, possibility 29
thirdness notion 82
time, abstract notions 50
tiny books, creation , *74–75*, 75
toilet-mother, role 76
toilet usage, fear 47
traffic light, granddaughter
    drawing *27*
tranquility, increase 36
transference: context 26;
    countertransference feeling,
    support 6
transference-countertransference
    dynamics 31
transferential-countertransferential
    movements 100
transferential elements, motivation 38
transgenerational depression,
    death 88
transgenerationality 68
treasures, attack (desires) 96
triangulation: myth 79;
    pyramidal triangulation 96;
    pyramid-oedipal-triangulation,
    imprisonment 92
true thoughts, protection 66
trusting relationship, development 31
Tustin, Frances 3

Twin Towers: patient consideration 55;
  plaque, drawing 55, *55*
"Two Principles" (Freud) 85

universe, creation 88
upside-down world, granddaughter drawing
  27, *29*
urethral sadistic phantasies 60
uterine atmosphere, sense 63

verbalizing, true free association 4
Virgil 29, 30

vitality, surge 35
volcano (eruption), warning
  (absence) 27

Winnicott, Donald Woods 3, 4
womb, return (phantasy) 59
womb-tomb association 88
work (mental health axis) 62
world, creation 88

zonal confusion,
  appearance 73

For Product Safety Concerns and Information please contact our EU
representative GPSR@taylorandfrancis.com
Taylor & Francis Verlag GmbH, Kaufingerstraße 24, 80331 München, Germany